Communities & Consequences II

Rebalancing New Hampshire's Human Ecology

By Peter Francese and Lorraine Stuart Merrill

Published by
Peter E. Randall Publisher
Portsmouth, NH
2020

ISBN: 978-1-942155-33-1
Library of Congress Control Number: 2019920443

Published by
Peter E. Randall Publisher
Box 4726
Portsmouth, NH 03802
www.perpublisher.com

Cover art by Bruce Jones: www.bwjonesart.com

We are extremely grateful for the organizations and individuals that have provided both financial and editorial support for this book and the complementary documentary by Jay Childs. We are also deeply appreciative for the assistance and expertise provided by our partner and fiscal agent New Hampshire PBS. Major contributing organizations are listed by level of sponsorship:

Dartmouth Hitchcock Medical Center

Cathartes

DTC Lawyers, PLLC

EnviroVantage

Heritage Plumbing,
Heating, Cooling, Electric

Exeter Hospital

New Hampshire
Electric Cooperative

New Hampshire REALTORS

Anagnost Companies

Hitchiner Manufacturing Co., Inc.

Orbit Group

Northeast Delta Dental

Chinburg Properties

We also wish to thank all the many individuals across New Hampshire who agreed to be interviewed for this book and the documentary. They provided technical guidance, and the human faces of the demographic facts about our state. We especially want to thank Steve Duprey, Sarah Currier, Dick Anagnost, Jeff Gowan, Steve Whitman, Joanne Cassulo, Steve Reno, Ben Gaetjens-Oleson, Sarah Wrightsman, Will Stewart and Hanna Flanders for generously sharing their time and expertise.

Contents

Introduction

Back in 1990, New Hampshire's age profile mirrored that of the nation. The state's median age of 32.7 was virtually the same as the United States' median of 32.8 years. One in four residents of both the nation and New Hampshire were under age 18, and one in five residents were 55 or older. The portion of New Hampshire's population in the prime working years of 18 to 55 was actually slightly higher than the national average.

But in the three decades since 1990, the picture has changed dramatically. The United States median age is now 38.2 years—and New Hampshire has gone from twenty-eighth-oldest median age to its current status as second-oldest state, with a median age of 43. Over these 30 years, New Hampshire's median age rose at a faster rate than any other state except Maine, and only Maine's median is higher, at 44.9 years. Vermont ranks third, at 42.8, and has started a "remote worker grant program" offering $10,000 grants to lure full-time employees from other states to move to Vermont. Northern New England is aging, growing very slowly, and experiencing difficulty attracting or retaining young people.

Some of this demographic predicament is self-inflicted. Unintended consequences of decisions and policy-making based on several persistent myths have together fundamentally altered the age structure of residents of our state. New Hampshire's seriously unbalanced age profile is not just some abstruse demographic quirk. It has serious social and economic consequences. Widespread worker shortages and rapidly declining school enrollments are among the more significant consequences. The very rapid increase in the elderly population without the accompanying workforce growth to provide the services that population requires is also resulting in serious social and economic consequences.

The population bulge we call the Baby Boom is reaching Social Security age and beyond. Impacts of the aging of this large demographic cohort are seen nationwide, but New Hampshire and northern New England are suffering far more severe demographic imbalance. Here the ranks of seniors are increasing even more rapidly—accompanied by shrinking numbers of younger adults and children. This unbalancing of the region's human ecology has resulted in fewer children in our schools, fewer students entering and graduating from colleges and universities, and widespread worker shortages.

With unemployment rates among the lowest in the nation, workforce shortages have afflicted every economic sector. This combination of swelling numbers of older people and dwindling numbers of the young may pinch hardest in healthcare and eldercare. Concerning Maine families struggling to secure eldercare, the August 14, 2019, *Washington Post* reported:

> The disconnect between Maine's aging population and its need for young workers to care for that population is expected to be mirrored in states throughout the country over the coming decade, demographic experts say...

And that's especially true in states with populations with fewer immigrants, who are disproportionately represented in many occupations serving the elderly, statistics show.

Nursing homes are closing. Those still in business have wait lists. As in neighboring Maine, New Hampshire families struggle to find home health aides, and assisted living and nursing homes vie with each other to fill staffing vacancies.

Shrinking school and college enrollments across New Hampshire and the region offer little hope for quick recovery. Contributing factors include high and rising costs of housing as well as high public college tuitions—which result in some of the highest average student loan debt loads in the country. New Hampshire college graduates in 2019 averaged $34,415 in student debt, compared to the national average of $28,650. Those debt levels can drive young graduates to other regions with higher wages or lower costs of living, especially housing.

Widespread opposition to housing types favored by and affordable to younger people and working families as well as weak state support for K-12 and public higher education both send signals of inhospitality to young people and families. Of all 50 states, New Hampshire has the highest rate of graduating high-school seniors choosing to attend college out of state—and the majority do not return.

■ Some Communities Start to Correct Course

Residents in towns and cities across the state are seeing the consequences of this imbalance, and they are beginning to join forces across generations and social classes to find solutions in their own communities. Young and old are working together to preserve and repurpose historic buildings for multiple uses, including youth-inspired and community-focused businesses and apartments available to all ages for workers, retirees, young

The Project:
Communities & Consequences II

Communities & Consequences II: Rebalancing New Hampshire's Human Ecology is a project that includes this book, a documentary film, and a series of statewide discussion forums. The project was created by the authors and filmmaker Jay Childs as the sequel to their earlier book and film completed in 2008. That first work was titled, *Communities & Consequences: The Unbalancing of New Hampshire's Human Ecology and What We Can Do About It*. For this sequel, the team traveled the state to report on innovative ideas and actions being taken to make more room for young people and to build thriving, multi-generational communities. Updates, including graphs and data, will be posted on the project website: www.nhpbs.org/communitiesandconsequences.

professionals. Local governments and boards are updating or creating new master plans, refocusing priorities, and ensuring that their ordinances and rules support their goals for more inclusive communities. (Look for more information, tools and resources in the Appendix: Resource Toolkit.)

This book is part of a larger project that includes a documentary film of the same title for NHPBS, set for a series of public screenings and discussion forums around the state. We describe the bumpy economic path our state has taken and how we got here. We highlight how Granite Staters are using innovative strategies to create more vibrant and welcoming communities for people of all generations, backgrounds, and walks of life. We hope the stories of these folks—our neighbors—create awareness and inspire others to join forces to create their own thriving communities for residents of all ages and backgrounds in all quarters of our state.

Exeter artist Bruce Jones created the cover image for this book, representing the collaborative intergenerational effort of rebalancing our human ecology. Ordinary New Hampshire residents are gently nudging the Granite State back into a balance where people of all ages and backgrounds are welcome so our communities and state can flourish in a bright future.

This book—along with the documentary, forums, and website—will provide examples of some of the best, most innovative ideas Granite Staters are using to address the imbalances in our human ecology. We want to express our appreciation and thanks to all the communities, individuals, and business and civic leaders who have generously shared their experiences and ideas. Our hope is that their stories will inspire more individuals and communities to join together and take the next steps to rebalance our state, support our families, rejuvenate our workforce, strengthen our communities, and establish a more economically sustainable path into the future.

Three Decades of Favoring the Old

1

The results are in on New Hampshire's 30-year experiment with age-based preferences. Over these three decades, the state's age distribution has diverged sharply from the national trend. Since 1990, the population of the United States has grown an average of 1.1% per year, while New Hampshire grew more slowly, by just 0.8% per year. This period coincided with the aging of the population bulge known as the Baby Boom into the over-55 age brackets. Chart 1 shows that from 1990 to 2018 the number of residents age 55 or older increased 77% nationally—but more than doubled in New Hampshire. Over the same period, the number of children under 18 in New Hampshire declined by 7%, compared to the nationwide *increase* of 16%.

The numbers for people in the prime working years of 25 to 55 reveal the reason for the acute labor shortages affecting all sectors of the New Hampshire economy. This cohort grew 21% nationwide since 1990—but barely edged up 2% in New Hampshire.

New Hampshire is one of the 10 smallest states in the US, with 1.4 million year-round residents—about the same number of people as the city of Dallas, Texas. But New Hampshire really

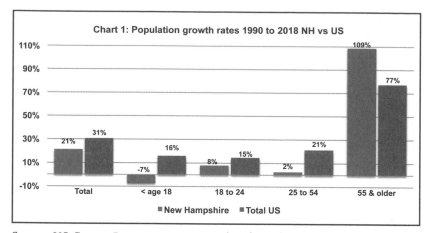

Source: US Census Bureau 1990 Census data & 2018 Census Bureau estimates

stands out in the change in the age structure of its population. In 1990, our state's age profile was about the same as the nation as a whole. However, since 1990, New Hampshire's age profile has diverged profoundly. The most significant example is the ratio of school-age children to residents aged 65 or older. Nationally, children five to 17 outnumber seniors by about 6%. In stark contrast, New Hampshire has 22% more senior residents age 65 or older than children the ages of five to 17.

■ Competition for Affordable Housing

New Hampshire's demographic imbalance is demonstrably much greater than can be accounted for by the aging of the Baby Boom generation. Other factors have contributed to the shortages of children and young people and to the growth in the over-55 age brackets. Housing is a major factor, in both cost and availability. Land and buildings are expensive, especially in sought-after regions of the state. Those tend to be areas with the most jobs; schools with better reputations; and scenic, recreational, and cultural amenities that attract tourists, second-home owners, and retirees. Many towns lack municipal water and sewer systems, requiring more land per dwelling and ruling out denser, more efficient development.

Russ Thibeault, of Applied Economic Research in Laconia, estimated for the NH Housing Finance Authority in 2019 that New Hampshire is short by about 20,000 housing units, including about 15,000 ownership units. But only 3,000–3,500 units are built each year. Towns are leery of new residential development because of fears of school-related property-tax increases. That's why many New Hampshire communities have used incentives to encourage construction of housing restricted to age 55 and up. Towns have effectively telegraphed, "Young people and families need not apply."

The attributes that make the state such a great place to live and raise a family—if only it were affordable—also draw tourists, second-home owners, and retirees from other states. The Granite State stands out for its share of housing stock that is seasonal- or occasional-use homes—which exacerbates the shortage and high cost of housing. This prevalence of second homes is most significant in the northern and lakes regions, but also exists in other tourism areas. In the three northernmost counties, more than one in four homes are occupied only on an occasional basis, as either second homes or tourist rentals.

This matters for purposes of estimating populations or taking a census, because the US Census Bureau only counts people in housing units occupied year-round. For example, Carroll County is estimated to have 48,800 residents living year-round in 21,200 households. Yet the actual number of dwelling units in the county is 41,200, or nearly twice that number, because 17,400 units (42%) are only occasionally occupied. This leaves fewer homes available at affordable prices for a family or individual employed in Carroll County. Employees of local businesses and other local residents must compete with buyers of vacation homes, who can push selling prices and rental rates beyond what households dependent on the local economy can afford.

For working families and young people in tourist areas like the Mount Washington Valley, the conundrum of finding affordable housing is compounded even further. Housing options for year-round residents are reduced by high demand and prices for vacation homes, or Airbnb and other short-term rental programs. Victoria Laracy, executive director of the Mount Washington Valley Housing Coalition, notes that, since 2010, rental rates for two-bedroom apartments in the Mount Washington Valley have increased 18%, while wages have increased only 5.5% over the same period. The vacancy rate for those two-bedroom apartments is essentially zero, she reports, while vacancy rates for other rentals hover around 1%. In this tight market, rentals that are available are not affordable to our workforce, Laracy adds. Many former long-term rentals are now rented for short terms and higher rates via services like Airbnb. "We do not have the available housing stock to bring young families and young workers to the valley," Laracy laments.

> Older and aging residents need a broad array of healthcare and other services. People 65 and older have increased 38% since 2010, while all other age groups have declined.

Worse still, average wages in local tourism-related businesses are lower than those in other areas of the state. Most towns in the area are too thinly populated to provide municipal water and sewer lines that could support more affordable development. Carroll County has become the oldest and fastest-aging county in New Hampshire. The county's median age of 53 is a full 10 years older than the state median.

Regional business and healthcare leaders have joined forces through the Mount Washington Valley Housing Coalition to address the increasingly urgent need for housing for workers to meet the needs of the fast-growing elderly and retired population. Older and aging residents need a broad array of healthcare and other services. People 65 and older have increased 38% since 2010, while all other age groups have declined. "By 2030, almost half of our community, our current workforce, will be over the age of 65," Laracy says. "With the lack of available housing, who is going to move here and fill those jobs?"

Carroll County is the most extreme case of how seasonal-home buyers and short-term rentals reduce housing affordability. This impact is felt in other counties or local markets where high percentages of homes are not primary residences. For example, 30% of the houses in Belknap County and 27% of those in Grafton County are seasonal or occasional-use dwellings.

■ Unintended Consequences: State Tax Policy Meets Local Development Policy

Stagnant numbers of working-age residents are a critical issue throughout the state when matched against the needs of the rapidly increasing elderly population—requiring ever more complex and labor-intensive emergency, healthcare, and support services. Workforce shortages have become the limiting factor on the state's economy. Yet many New Hampshire towns have compounded the problem by using generous incentives to encourage housing development restricted to older residents only. Even worse, towns have discouraged construction of much needed housing for the workers who could provide services for the fast-rising numbers of older residents.

Development regulations designed by municipalities to favor housing for older residents over housing available to all ages have yielded the desired results—along with a heavy burden of unintended consequences. The preference for elderly housing over family housing was not intended to ensure shortages of vital workers and service providers. It was more about fears of the cost of schools—rooted in New Hampshire's reliance on the property tax to finance public education, and memories of rapid growth in parts of the state in the 1980s.

With no broad-based state sales or income tax, towns and cities in New Hampshire must rely primarily on local property taxes to pay for public schools. To avoid new or increased state taxes, in the last decade the legislature has reduced state funding to towns for pensions and infrastructure—effectively shifting those costs to local property taxpayers. The property tax on real estate is also the one revenue stream directly controlled by local voters. Many voters have come to associate families and children with higher school costs and higher taxes. Some residents have felt the only way to hold down their property-tax bills was to control the types of housing constructed in their town. They would block or discourage housing suitable for families with children—while encouraging restricted-age units to expand the property-tax base.

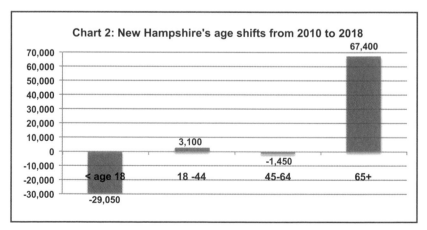

Source: Census Bureau estimates
The consequences of local policies that favor the elderly and discourage families with children.

■ Deflating the Myth That Housing Inflates School Costs

Russ Thibeault, of Applied Economic Research in Laconia, authored a front-page article in the September 26, 2019, *New Hampshire Business Review* titled, "Where have all the children gone?" Thibeault began the article thus:

> One of the most, if not the very most, pervasive and inaccurate myths I encounter in my work around the state is the false belief that every new housing unit will generate "at least" two public school students. You could say that this is one of the anthems of the NIMBY subculture.
>
> This red flag is often hoisted up the flagpole at planning board and zoning board meetings across the state—and it has been so for several decades. The inaccurate fear is that local schools will be inundated with new students who overcrowd classrooms, drain local tax coffers and generate sharply rising tax rates.

Thibeault then proceeds to dismantle this stubborn myth. He notes that New Hampshire Department of Education data, tracking enrollment trends at the state and local levels, "shows unmistakably that enrollment in New Hampshire's public schools is consistently falling, a trend that began to surface about 20 years ago and is continuing through today."

Thibeault says enrollment began dropping around 2000, primarily because Baby Boomers' children had moved on to college age, overall population growth had slowed, and birth rates were declining. "The math of it all is quite transparent," he wrote. "Even an economist can figure out that if enrollment is declining while we are adding new units then the enrollment per occupied unit must be declining. And it is."

Since 2000, New Hampshire has gained 68,200 new occupied housing units, but school enrollment is down by more than 31,000. Thibeault says an occupied housing unit in New Hampshire now generates an average of 0.33 students.

Applied Economic Research did a study for the NH Housing Finance Authority in 2012 that determined average school enrollments for different types of housing. Single-family detached houses averaged 0.48 students; multi-family housing of five or more units averaged 0.17; and manufactured housing averaged 0.26 students. In the five years since this analysis was completed, school enrollments have fallen by 5 percent. Thibeault concludes with his own warning to New Hampshire communities:

> In New Hampshire's current environment of slow growth, an aging population and very low birth rates, many communities would be well advised to encourage more housing construction, else they face the unpalatable option of closing neighborhood and local community schools because of unsustainably low enrollment.
>
> An inaccurate understanding of the relationship between new housing and school enrollment engenders and perpetuates inappropriate growth policies that stymie new construction at a time when we need more housing and, in many districts, more students. Fear of rising enroll-ment is passé for nearly every school district in the state. It is a legacy concern, dating back to the last period of rising enrollment, nearly 30 years ago.

Richard England, University of New Hampshire professor emeritus of economics and nationally recognized expert on property tax and local public finance, analyzed housing growth, student enrollment, achievement, and education property tax rates for the state and all its municipalities. The conclusion of his 21-page report summed it up this way:

[T]his report seeks to answer a very simple question, that is nonetheless a very important one: Will the construction of new homes in a community and the additional enrollment of children in its public schools necessarily raise the property tax rate? Using three types of analysis, I believe I have shown that the answer is definitely not.

■ What Do New Housing Units Bring to Town?

The facts about falling school enrollments and the costs of operating schools tell a different story. Town planning and zoning boards, and the members of the public who fill their hearing rooms and elect the board members in many towns, all need accurate information on these complex issues as they consider approving housing projects.

NH Housing Finance Authority research shows that 50 new homes are likely to bring no more than 12 to 24 children into the local schools, depending on type of housing. Over a typical four-to-five-year build-out period, that would mean an average of less than one additional child per grade each year. In districts where school enrollment has been declining, those 50 new homes would most likely result in no additional school expenses at all. A more likely impact of 50 new housing units would be to put between 75 and 100 adults into the local workforce and perhaps opening new businesses—as well as shopping in local stores, using local service providers, and eating in area restaurants.

Consider the gains, not just the costs from retaining and attracting more young people. Research conducted by the University System of New Hampshire in 2007 determined that 323 additional college graduates would need to stay in the state after graduation just to increase the percentage of graduates that remain in New Hampshire from 50% to 55%. The USNH study projected this change would have a positive economic impact for the state of $19 million a year. Over five years, the cumulative impact of retaining at least 55% of new graduates would be over $290 million. Housing that is affordable for people of all ages creates far more in economic benefits than any marginal costs to the community in providing educational or other municipal services.

■ A Closer Look at Declining School Enrollments

The New Hampshire Department of Education's most recent (2018) enrollment report shows long-term decline in the number of students at all grade levels, for both public and private schools. Over the past 10 years, public pre-K through high-school enrollments have fallen by 10%, resulting in about 20,600 fewer students. Over the same decade, private schools enrolled 2,900 fewer students in the same grades—a 15% reduction.

Enrollments in a majority of New Hampshire school districts may appear pretty stable over the 10 years from 2008–2018, with 91 of 162 districts either gaining or losing fewer than 100 students each. But for smaller districts, those smaller numerical losses can be devastating. School Administrative Unit 7—comprising the small Coos County towns of Colebrook, Clarksville, Pittsburg, and Stewartstown—lost 30% of its student population in that time. For Pittsburg, 59 fewer students represents more than 40% decline.

In 2019, SAU 7 began merger talks with the Essex North Supervisory Union across the Connecticut River in Canaan, Vermont, which has lost 40% of its students over the last 15 years. "We have 220 high schoolers going to three high schools in the region," SAU 7 Superintendent Bruce Beasley said in an interview with NH Public Radio. "Many community members feel there is a better way to provide a better education to these students." If these talks move forward, it would create the third interstate school district spanning the Connecticut

River boundary with Vermont. Some schools would close, with accompanying losses of community tradition and identity.

Sixty-two districts lost between 100 and 1,000 students over the past decade, and another five larger districts saw enrollments decline by 1,000 students or more. A closer look at those five— which are all growing in population—reveals a pattern. The five school districts losing more than 1,000 students include four of New Hampshire's largest municipalities: Manchester, Nashua, Salem, and Londonderry. The fifth is Timberlane, a regional district of five towns on the Massachusetts border. Manchester's enrollment decline is partly attributable to the decision of voters in Bedford, an adjacent affluent suburb, to build their own high school and cease sending grade 9–12 students to Manchester. Bedford's withdrawal explains about half of Manchester's lost enrollment.

The puzzle of the other four districts' big enrollment declines as populations were rising can be explained by the large numbers of new dwelling units restricted to residents ages 55 or older. Their rise in population coinciding with school enrollment decline can be attributed almost entirely to their favoring of senior homeowners. These cities and towns rank among the state's highest for numbers of age-restricted housing units, with a combined total over 4,200—along with 2,200 generous senior property-tax exemptions.

Housing policy choices favoring the elderly leave many fewer dwelling units available for families with children, resulting in sharply declining school enrollments. Nashua alone provides property-tax exemptions to more than 800 older homeowners. These districts are seeing population growth— but entirely among older people without children.

Shrinking enrollments can pose greater challenges for schools than growth. Closures and consolidation of schools and reductions in staff—even just uncertainty and insecurity around potential closures and staff reductions—erode staff and community morale.

"Losing your high school identity—the sports, the mascot—is part of the conversation," Karen Conroy, superintendent of the Canaan, Vermont, district explained to NHPR about the proposal to merge with NH SAU 7 and consolidate from three high schools down to one. "But we are trying to pull together to see what we can offer." Conroy, who previously served as a superintendent in New Hampshire's North Country, said the main goal in merging districts is to improve academic offerings to students.

■ Local Control, Regional Impact

Town-by-town decisions to keep out "affordable housing" for everybody except residents aged 55 and up have contributed to severe regional worker shortages. The concept of "local control" is deeply ingrained in New England, where each town has primary responsibility for providing municipal services such as police and fire departments, libraries and public schools. In many states outside the Northeast, public schools are governed at the county level. In another part of the country, New Hampshire would likely have a dozen public school districts—one for each county plus probably two more for the state's two largest cities.

But the Granite State, with 283 municipalities, has 162 school districts. Some towns have banded together to form cooperative or regional entities to provide some or all levels of public education, including 62 middle schools and 73 high schools. But over the last two decades more of these collaborative arrangements have been splitting up than forming. These divorces and failed attempts at forming cooperative districts often result from disparities in wealth or local tax bases, as well as disagreements over apportionment of costs and levels of services and spending. For years, fear of school costs has driven local planning and development decisions across the state.

■ The Myth of the Average Per-pupil School Cost

Perhaps the most widely quoted number in New Hampshire is the average cost per pupil for public education. The New Hampshire Department of Education publishes the numbers each year for each school district, calculated to two decimal places. The 2018 (most recent available) state average cost per pupil was $15,865.26.

Average cost varies substantially by district. Manchester, the state's largest city and largest school district with about 13,500 students, has the lowest cost per child at $12,024.13. The smallest of all full K-12 districts in the state is Sunapee, which with just over 400 students charts the highest costs per child at $25,435.73—more than twice that of Manchester.

> The popular focus on cost per pupil has created the myth that operating a public-school system is a variable cost dependent only on the number of children.

Over the five years from 2013 to 2018, the statewide average cost per pupil rose almost 18%. But in this same time, enrollments decreased 4.3%. If enrollments had increased or held steady, statewide costs per child would have risen much more slowly, at approximately the rate of inflation.

School costs can deceptively appear to be spiking in a small school district with declining enrollments, when in fact they are changing very slowly. The popular focus on cost per pupil has created the myth that operating a public-school system is a variable cost dependent only on the number of children. In reality, operation of a school or an entire school district is a largely fixed set of costs. Adding or subtracting a few children per grade does not materially change the total expense of providing public education.

This common but false narrative predicting huge property-tax impacts has often resulted in fierce opposition to any proposed new housing open to families with children. Multi-unit apartments seem to draw the most opposition, although they generally produce fewer children. Apartments are in short supply. About two-thirds of all housing in New Hampshire consists of one dwelling unit on a lot of varying size, but generally an acre (43,560 square feet) or more, sometimes much more.

■ "We've kind of done this to ourselves"

Housing in New Hampshire was the topic on NH Public Radio's *The Exchange* on April 25, 2018, part of NHPR's "Balance" series on "The costs, benefits and trade-offs of living in NH." Program host Laura Knoy asked Jeff Feingold, editor of the *New Hampshire Business Review*, how important zoning and code regulations are in making it so hard to get the kinds of housing people need in the state. Zoning and development regulations at the local level are a major reason we don't have very affordable housing, Feingold said, adding:

> Over the years we built those houses on our two-acre lot minimums and other things that have been very restrictive in communities...Many towns have willfully set up their regulations to keep out what we would call affordable housing, workforce housing, multifamily housing... We've seen this happening over many, many years in New Hampshire—that communities have been using zoning regulations to basically block certain people from coming.

But while these exclusionary regulations have been going on for years, he notes some communities are starting to reverse

Definitions

AFFORDABLE HOUSING is housing which is deemed affordable to those with the state median household income or below. From their 2018 survey, the Census Bureau estimated the median household income for New Hampshire was $75,000. That means half the state's households have an income equal to or less than that figure. At that median income, a home costing $300,000 or less is considered affordable.

WORKFORCE HOUSING is permanent year-round housing available to households regardless of age and best provided near places of employment. Workforce housing can include, but is not limited to, subsidized and affordable housing, as well as market-rate and mixed-income housing. It includes a variety of housing types suitable for households with different needs and income levels, for both owners and renters, to meet the needs of families and individuals who represent the majority of New Hampshire's diverse workforce. New Hampshire RSA 674:58-:61, the state's workforce housing law, defines income and affordability ranges.

course, and supporting more density of housing, often in conjunction with mixed-use development.

"In the long term we've kind of done this to ourselves," Feingold said of New Hampshire's demographic predicament and housing crisis. He said he has heard a lot from builders about how restrictive regulations are in communities all over the state. "It's a huge contributing factor to the state we're in right now in terms of housing. We need higher density housing—more efficient land use."

In a subsequent telephone interview, Feingold emphasized that towns have used inefficient and burdensome land-use regulations—such as large minimum-lot sizes and setbacks, and excessive parking requirements—as tools to prevent construction of housing for certain ages and income groups. These inefficient development regulations are also environmentally detrimental, wasting land and unnecessarily increasing impervious surfaces that degrade water quality.

Feingold and his wife sold their long-time home in New London and moved into one of 110 apartments in a dense, mixed-use development in Manchester's Millyard. Now he walks to the NHBR offices instead of commuting and marvels each day at the sight in his neighborhood of "hundreds of young people going to work!" Proof, he suggests, that this is the kind of environment where young people want to live and work.

Labor shortages are now costing towns and cities more money to entice people to fill vital staff positions. In August 2019, the Bedford Police Department announced it was finally able to fill some of its critical 20% vacant positions by offering a number of new incentives—like higher wages for new officers and $10,000 signing bonuses. News reports abound of fire departments around the state struggling with shortages of both professional (paid) and volunteer firefighters and emergency medical technicians.

■ Local Regulations Favor Sprawl

Municipal land-use and building regulations often favor senior residents—intentionally or unintentionally. Young individuals, couples starting out, or other working-age people often cannot afford or do not wish to buy the expensive single-family homes on large lots that predominate in most New Hampshire communities. Proposals to build more compact homes on smaller acreages or multi-unit residential housing that would better meet their needs face a number of stringent zoning, site-plan review, and other requirements relating to minimum lot sizes, setbacks, numbers of units per acre, parking, and more.

Even without promoting or rewarding restricted-age housing, zoning and stringent building code regulations still inflate the costs of building or owning a home. Until the legislature first adopted a state building code in 2002, it was a local option. Code requirements for a certificate of occupancy eliminated a traditional affordability option of living in a home while completing construction in stages. Zoning that requires large lots with wide setbacks dramatically pumps up the cost for a buildable lot. Developers explain that it is not economical to build a modest or smaller-size home on a big, expensive lot. In many towns, zoning mandates the kinds of residential development patterns defined as urban or suburban sprawl.

■ Large Lots Do *Not* Preserve Rural Character or Open Space

Zoning in many towns requires lot sizes of two acres or more for new dwellings. Such large-lot requirements are based on the misguided belief that larger lots will preserve rural character, conserve open space, and support local agriculture. In reality, large lots waste land and create suburban sprawl by converting more, not less, open land to development per unit. Towns end up spending more to maintain longer roads. Science-based alternatives such as lot-size-by-soil-type make more efficient use of natural resources by determining the minimum acreage necessary for an approved on-lot septic system and well.

Affordable housing opponents rationalize that big homes on big lots will be priced too high for young families. Or at least the tax yield from such expensive dwellings would cover any school costs. Opposition to housing that would be more affordable for younger people and families has been codified into prohibitive zoning restrictions, and any waivers too often reserved for age-restricted developments.

During the discussion on that April 25, 2018, *The Exchange* program on NHPR, host Laura Knoy shared an observation with her panel of guests. "It is kind of stunning to think about, you know, planners looking at that and saying, 'Ooh, we don't want too many kids,'" she said, "when every single week practically, somebody comes into the studio and says 'Workforce! Workforce! Workforce! Please bring in young families.'"

Urgent Care for Communities

2

Rather than a drain on tax dollars, children and young people represent current and future growth and vitality for our towns and state. Everyone can participate in helping to rebalance New Hampshire's age profile to recharge communities and fill the thousands of job vacancies produced by the strong economy and the needs of the growing numbers of older residents. Urgent care for our communities starts with busting the myths described in chapter 1, and identifying and taking positive steps to create communities that are inviting for all ages. The work involves removing roadblocks to creating more diverse housing choices and welcoming communities. The need is urgent—before our out-of-kilter demographics further harm prospects for workforce growth, economic vitality, and healthy communities.

"The more we can all do as individuals, towns, organizations, employers, and community groups to make people feel more welcome," advises Will Stewart, executive director of Stay Work Play New Hampshire, "the more we can help people feel they *belong*." This advice applies to nuts-and-bolts actions like changing zoning to support more affordable housing options and more vibrant communities. Personal acts of kindness to newcomers are also important, along with efforts to reach out and encourage more diverse members of the community to participate in local governance and organizations. "Bring back the Welcome Wagon!" Stewart suggests.

Stay Work Play NH, Inc. (SWP) was established in 2009 as a nonprofit organization to advance efforts begun in 2007 by a coalition of the University System of New Hampshire (USNH), major employers, and newly formed regional networks of young professionals. These leaders from higher education and business were keenly aware of the demographic writing on the wall—the looming steep declines in potential students and graduates. The state was then fourth-oldest in the nation and many Baby Boomers were close to retirement. Employers were having trouble finding skilled workers. Half of college-bound graduating high school seniors were choosing colleges outside the state, and college graduates were leaving the state at too high a rate to meet projected employment needs, especially for skilled workers.

Also in the spring of 2009, the Governor's Task Force on Young Worker Retention released its report recommending creation of an independent organization to establish a website (StayWorkPlay.org) and marketing effort to promote all that New Hampshire has to offer to 20- to 30-year-olds. Leaders from USNH, the NH College and University Council, the Business and Industry Association of NH, the NH High Technology Council, and the NH Department of Resources and Economic Development incorporated SWP. For more than a decade, state and regional groups have understood the gravity of New Hampshire's demographics. But that urgency has not translated to the local level—to the voters who can move the levers for change.

Will Stewart is an example of the demographic SWP is trying to attract. Starting his career in journalism, he came to

New Hampshire from Tennessee in 2004 at the age of 25 to take a job as a reporter with Hippo Press in Manchester. Now 40 and "[with] a kid in the local schools, an elected office (alderman) in Manchester, and leading SWP," he says, "I am rooted here for sure!"

"Young people today, perhaps more so than previous generations, really value the ability to make a difference and an impact, both in their professional and personal lives," Stewart maintains. He thinks this is key to distinguishing the Granite State from the competition. "I would argue that New Hampshire is a place, perhaps more than other, more populous places," he says, "where a young person can make a real difference in less time, and with less resources than would be required in bigger places."

Showcasing opportunities to make a difference is a new strategic priority for SWP, which held its first annual "Summit for Young Changemakers," a sold-out event, in April 2019. The second summit, slated for April 2020, aims to draw young people aged 18–40 "who want to make the Granite State—or your corner of it—a better place." Stories in subsequent chapters of this book offer examples of how young people are contributing and becoming leaders in their local communities.

■ Sending Messages

Citizens of all ages can come together to create master plans for their communities—developing a vision and identifying community values, priorities, and goals. However, as shown in the story of Lancaster's revitalization in chapter 3, municipal leaders often then find that their town's ordinances and codes conflict with and impede the values, goals, directions, and vision articulated by the community's master plan or other policy work.

Communities with long traditions of strong civic values— where generations of families have lived and participated and volunteered in town government and local organizations—have found themselves, perhaps with good intentions, voting for age-discriminatory zoning. With rising property taxes causing hardship for all property owners of limited means, they have enacted exemptions for one age group and shifted the balance onto all others, including younger taxpayers. They may allow heated rhetoric against any proposed housing construction other than large single-family homes on large lots to dominate planning and zoning board debates. These conflicted community actions have lasting community, regional, and even statewide consequences.

Every town or city vote to increase elderly tax exemptions, or provide affordable housing only for seniors, sends a clear message to young people. Public expressions of bitter opposition to any affordable workforce housing proposals send the same message to aspiring young people and others who work in our communities: "We don't want you here because we think your presence will increase our property taxes and lower our property values." Sometimes the messages are even worse—"We don't want that kind of people."

We can stop sending those messages—or at least add stronger countervailing voices in support of inclusion, regardless of age, background, or income level. We can engage more young residents in community life and governance. Unfortunately, young people don't vote in local elections for town offices or zoning ordinance changes nearly as often as older people do. And the meaning and impact of ballot warrant articles of amendment to zoning ordinances are often indecipherable to voters of any age who lack experience and knowledge of zoning language.

But many young people have been voting with their feet— leaving for other towns and other states where they can more readily find a place. And the younger people who aspire to be part of our communities—to buy or rent starter condos or homes in our towns—have no vote because they are not residents.

■ Local Taxes, Regional Workforce Impact

Most other states finance public education primarily at the state and/or county level, rather than by property-tax payers in small towns. The Granite State's tax structure and school-finance system localizes the costs, but not the benefits, of sustaining a healthy, diverse demographic mix. Smaller towns also often lack the wherewithal to fund sewer and water infrastructure needed to support housing density that allows for greater affordability of housing. That infrastructure can also support higher-value commercial development to beef up the local tax base.

Decisions are made and costs are borne at the local municipal level. But businesses and employers throughout the surrounding region bear the costs of the resulting labor shortages. If businesses cannot grow or even maintain existing staffing and operation levels, taxpayers' chickens may come home to roost. Those businesses may choose to expand elsewhere or pull up stakes and move to greener workforce pastures, leaving local taxpayers in the lurch.

The Governor's Millennial Advisory Council (GMAC) is organized into four policy area subcommittees representing their generation's values and priorities for their communities and state. The 2017 annual report listed recommendations for each of those four policy areas: Housing, Workforce Development, Education, and Conservation/Environment/Transportation. The GMAC's 2017 annual report linked the state's tax structure to the affordable housing crisis—and specifically to the inability of younger workers to compete for housing with more affluent retirees flocking to New Hampshire from other states for the tax advantages. From the community and economic development section on page 9 of the report:

Attracting and retaining businesses relies on a young professional workforce. Businesses need a variety of housing options to accommodate their employees' needs. Currently, businesses in New Hampshire are facing workforce development challenges that are intertwined with the lack of affordable, quality housing for young professionals.

The current tax structure poses a challenge. Since there is an emphasis on property tax and no income tax, wealthier people are seeking out New Hampshire from other parts of New England to relocate or retire to, driving overall housing rates up. This, in turn, makes it difficult for young people just starting out in their careers to afford housing and the cost of property taxes in New Hampshire.

■ Should We Stay or Should We Go?

Stay Work Play commissioned a survey in December 2017 of 20–40-year-olds in New Hampshire. The purpose was to identify reasons they choose to live in New Hampshire; evaluate their satisfaction with living here; determine how young residents rate the quality of life in New Hampshire; and see if they plan to remain in the state.

Fifty-nine percent said they were satisfied with New Hampshire, but 30% said they were likely to leave. Top-ranking reasons to stay included: quality of environment, quality of parks and recreational areas, sense of community or neighborhood, proximity to outdoor activities, safe place to live, and affordable taxes (except for property taxes).

Top reasons young professionals gave for leaving the state included: lack of affordable housing, lack of jobs and career opportunities, few opportunities to meet new people, lack of access to cultural opportunities, lack of access to affordable childcare, lack of public transportation, lack of cultural diversity, and lack of quality nightlife and entertainment.

The barriers to attracting and keeping young people have been known for more than a decade. The 2009 report of the Governor's Task Force for the Recruitment and Retention of a Young Workforce recommended more affordable housing, expanding commuter rail, increasing availability and afford- ability of quality childcare, and more. (Note: many communities make permitting and approval of childcare facilities, including in-home "family day-care" providers, extremely difficult and expensive.)

"But the big surprise in the survey," Will Stewart notes, "is the loneliness factor. Twenty-one percent said they had no friend close by or accessible." Isolation from family was also cited by one in four surveyed. New data from a national YouGov poll announced in August 2019 found that Millennials report feeling lonely much more often than their older Gen X and Baby Boomer counterparts. Thirty percent of Millennials said they always or often feel lonely—even more than the 21% in the SWP survey. In the YouGov poll just 20% of members of Generation X and 15% of Baby Boomers reported always or often feeling lonely. Possibly New Hampshire is not any lonelier than other states. But these responses show how important outreach and welcoming efforts may be for young people starting out in life.

■ What Kind of Housing Do Millennials Want?

Sarah Wrightsman is a young New Hampshire native who has chosen to stay in New Hampshire and focus her work on resolving the housing shortage and other challenges for young people. At 30, she is executive director of the Workforce Housing Coalition of the Greater Seacoast and housing planner for the Regional Economic Development Center. She co-hosts a podcast called Creative Guts, and blogs for StayWorkPlay.org. She loves living

Sarah Wrightsman, executive director of the Workforce Housing Coalition of the Greater Seacoast, works with residents participating in Pelham's housing planning charrette.

in downtown Durham, and is an alternate member of the planning board. Wrightsman enjoys hiking and other outdoor activities. Here are some excerpts from "Demystifying Millennials: What Type of Housing Do Millennials Want?" a blog she wrote (July 11, 2019) for StayWorkPlay.org, offering some advice for cities and towns:

> Even the smallest, most rural town can attract millennials to their community by providing quality housing affordable to them. Not the millennials seeking an urban nightlife, but those seeking a smaller, more rural town where they and their growing family can put down roots. Millennials, who turn 30 this year on average, are doing a lot of the normal things we expected them to do at 30. My younger brother is talking about buying a house, several of my close friends are engaged or recently married, a Facebook friend

is pregnant with her first kiddo, and a colleague just had her second. It isn't surprising that people in their thirties tend to seek a home they can afford, in a community with a good school system, within a reasonable commuting distance to their place of employment.

While there is nothing inherently wrong with "Millennial-driven" housing, like tiny houses, micro-units, co-housing, or living with your parents (sorry, parents!) — it is dangerous to believe any of these solutions are THE solution to housing affordability for all millennials. Some of us just want a regular house.

So, make room at the table because the millennials are here and we want to be heard. Let us choose where we'll put our roots down, and in what kind of housing. More than ever, millennials are stepping into leadership positions and that's good news because the discussion about what millennials want is better left to the millennials. But, there is a role for

> Regardless of how wonderful your community is, you will struggle to attract young people if they can't find a place to live.

communities: harness your strengths. Don't try to become something you're not—work on becoming the best, most welcoming version of what you already are. And ensure the infrastructure is there. Regardless of how wonderful your community is, you will struggle to attract young people if they can't find a place to live. Make it possible for the next generation to choose your town.

■ Choosing to Thrive, Not Wither

Rebalancing New Hampshire's human ecology starts with busting a few myths and convincing residents of towns and cities around the state they have nothing to fear from new residents who might have children. Children born in the twenty-first century deserve to be valued and taken seriously as the future of our communities and state—just as the Baby Boom children were in the 1950s and 1960s. Families are foundational building blocks of strong communities.

With over 250 separate town or city planning boards, this will be a long-term and continuing effort. Regional planning commissions, the NH Office of Strategic Initiatives, and the NH Housing Finance Authority all provide much information and training for local planners. (See the Appendix: Resource Toolkit for these and more.) Part of the rebalancing task is to show how towns and cities are not independent, isolated entities, but rather are all part of the interconnected web of communities and regions of our state and beyond.

Excluding young people and families with children may appear to have some short-term benefit to a town, but does long-term damage to the community and to the economic well being of the region and state. The severity of widespread labor shortages across the state is directly related to the unwillingness of individual communities to allow for housing growth, especially in the affordable categories. Chapter 6 tells how communities of the Upper Valley are working to address these challenges together as a region—across town and even state lines.

Garret Dash Nelson, a geography instructor at Dartmouth College who lived in Nashua during his teens, says the uneven geographic distribution of the benefits and burdens makes it hard for towns to cooperate regionally on affordable housing. In a presentation to a workforce housing group sponsored by the regional nonprofit Vital Communities, he showed how housing stock, rental vacancies, income levels, and jobs all vary across communities in the Upper Valley. He listed challenges but also pointed to existing legacy infrastructure and density in some towns as a regional strength.

New State Funding for Affordable Housing

The NH Housing Finance Authority will be able to support development of more affordable housing thanks to the 2020–21 state budget, which includes a $5 million annual commitment to the state's Affordable Housing Fund. This bipartisan effort addresses the legislature's finding that "An adequate supply of housing that is affordable to a range of incomes is essential to New Hampshire's economic and community development goals."

The Affordable Housing Fund—the state's housing trust fund administered by the NH Housing Finance Authority—was established in 1988 to provide low-interest loans and grants for the construction, rehabilitation, and/or acquisition of housing affordable to families and individuals with low to moderate incomes. The fund was established in 1988, but infrequent appropriations over 31 years have totaled just $17.6 million. The 2020–21 biennial budget includes a one-time $5 million general fund appropriation to the Affordable Housing Fund. Additionally, and for the first time, the legislature provided $5 million in annual dedicated funding from the real estate transfer tax beginning in 2021.

To reduce delays in the approval process for new housing projects, the New Hampshire legislature also established a Housing Appeals Board. The purpose of this board, slated to begin operation in 2020, is to create an alternative to Superior Court for appealing decisions of local planning, zoning and other boards. Legislators established the Housing Appeals Board under RSA 679.1 as, "an alternative track for review of local decisions on housing development without diminishing anyone's existing legal right to pursue a remedy in superior court and without affecting local control or changing the legal standards by which local decisions are adjudicated."

One way to convince communities they will benefit from residential growth is to show examples of places where growth has occurred with positive impacts for both the local and regional economy. Subsequent chapters highlight New Hampshire communities that have begun to welcome new residents of all ages and are seeing substantial economic and social benefits result.

■ Connecting the Demographic and Policy Dots

People of all ages and walks of life in communities across our state are beginning to connect these dots. Workforce shortages, housing shortages, property taxes, education costs, the exodus of young people, and the influx of seniors are all connected. Despite snowy winters, the Granite State has become a retirement mecca, thanks in part to New Hampshire's advantageous affordable housing and tax provisions earmarked exclusively for older people. With some of the highest public-college tuition rates, New Hampshire has long ranked at the bottom for state funding of all levels of public education. Despite draws of natural beauty, outdoor recreation, and down-to-earth culture, New Hampshire has not yet become a magnet for the young.

Dean Christon, executive director of the New Hampshire Housing Finance Authority, explains the situation this way:

> New Hampshire has experienced strong economic growth and low unemployment over the past 10 years. At the same time, the state's available housing stock is not meeting the needs of its residents, whatever their age.
>
> Those entering the workforce have difficulty finding affordable rental apartments, and young families—who are typically homebuyers looking for a "starter home" (generally under $300,000)—find themselves in a highly competitive market and often unable to afford newly constructed homes. At the same time, older residents of the

state who own larger homes are seeking different, more compact accommodations, with improved accessibility, lower maintenance, and proximity to services to reduce the need to drive.

Christon emphasizes:

> By encouraging communities to develop mixed-use housing, individuals and families of all ages and income levels can live and work together. New Hampshire communities become stronger with an intergenerational mix— where people choose to live, work, raise a family, and even retire in the same area.

■ Keene Creates Arts Corridor

Several cities and towns are making changes to appeal to current residents and newcomers, young and old alike. The city of Keene, Keene State College, and local nonprofits are working with the Monadnock Economic Development Corp. to reinvent a corridor currently dominated by parking lots and concrete through Keene's historic redbrick downtown as an arts corridor. Still in early planning stages, the vision includes a pedestrian mall with a new city welcome center and outdoor performance venue for concerts, meetings, and events like farmers markets. The idea builds on Keene's existing arts scene—which includes an arts cooperative and a series of 16 murals depicting the city's history on downtown building exteriors.

Innovative combined work and living spaces for artists are planned for an existing building. The affordable studio and living spaces would be available for artists already in the greater Keene community, and these units would help to attract new creative professionals to the city. Planners expect the concentration of artist studios and galleries to attract visitors and customers. Resident artists would enliven the downtown district throughout the day and evening.

In a July 13, 2019, editorial titled, "If we build it: Keene 'arts corridor' project has a lot of pluses, but much still to be figured out," the *Keene Sentinel* noted frequent complaints about the city are that it does not have enough jobs or growth, or enough business to offset resident taxes. "Keene's population has been stagnant and aging for the past several decades, and major employers have been slowly moving their jobs elsewhere," the editorial noted. "If this plan makes Keene a more attractive location for young workers to live, offering a more-rounded, vibrant cultural experience, it may serve as a draw for the skilled workers employers seek, and in turn spur business growth."

Arts also figure strongly in Littleton's famously revitalized downtown. Galleries and studios line the restored riverfront streets, and restaurants and cafes feature live music. The beautifully restored Littleton Opera House hosts ballet, concerts, and theater productions. Guiding a tour of the downtown for historic preservationists, 30-something Selectman Chad Stearns showed genuine love for his hometown and pride in what he and other younger-generation residents have been able to contribute as members of the community.

■ Franklin Plans White-water Recreation Park

While Keene expands its existing arts and cultural assets, the city of Franklin is looking to refurbish and capitalize on its natural heritage and outdoor recreation resources, with a strong nod to youth and active people of all ages. Outdoor recreational opportunities are a primary reason young people stay in NH, according to the Stay Work Play survey.

The plan would clean up the Winnipesaukee River's magnificent course through the city and create Mill City Park—the first white-water outdoor recreation park in the Northeast. The plan enhances and expands uses of this section of the river, an 11-acre land and water corridor favored by kayakers, and an easy walk from downtown and residential areas. Trails on both sides of the river will welcome walkers and mountain bikers. The historic urban landscape retains features from the hydro-powered industries that once lined the river. Permaculture design principles will guide the landscape of the new park, including an area of community gardens. A holistic permaculture approach uses ecological principles found in natural systems to design more sustainable, resilient human environments.

■ Upward Trends for Communities

Trend-spotters at the NH Office of Strategic Initiatives reported in September 2019 that among the 35 communities that had adopted master plan updates since the beginning of 2018, an increasing number are adopting chapters beyond those spelled out in the state's master plan statute, RSA 674:2. Emerging new master-plan topics include public health, agriculture, climate change, and the arts—all topics of concern and interest to many younger people.

Another trend for all of New England is the growing role of new Americans or immigrants in sustaining and revitalizing communities. (See sidebar: New Americans Helping to Strengthen Communities) "Lack of cultural diversity" was a common reason 20–40-year-old respondents to the Stay Work Play survey gave for deciding to leave New Hampshire. New Americans are adding diversity and vitality, making New Hampshire communities more attractive and engaging for people of all generations. Even with just 5 percent of its population born in other countries, New Hampshire is seeing benefits of increased cultural diversity in the arts, local restaurants featuring international cuisines, farming, markets, businesses, civic organizations, and more.

People take pride in creative, grassroots actions to revitalize their communities. Forward-looking town leaders and boards are taking a hard look at their master plans and zoning and sub-division rules, and they are listening to the needs and concerns of local employers and residents of all ages and income levels to meet changing needs. The next chapters explore some of those inspiring stories.

New Americans Helping to Strengthen Communities

"We have been blessed," Steve Duprey told *Communities & Consequences* documentary filmmaker Jay Childs. "Concord is—I'm biased I know—but I think it's one of the greatest communities. I think we have the largest number of refugees—new Americans—who've come to Concord. We were very fortunate to get involved very early on, and set up what I think is the largest job-training program by a private employer for new Americans." Duprey, president of Foxfire Property Management and The Duprey Companies, says just about every new American who comes to Concord is advised, "you should stop in at The Duprey Companies because they may have a job for you."

"We have a large percentage of our workforce who are new Americans," Duprey added. "We are extraordinarily proud of that fact; we are proud of them. They have made Concord a better community. They make the state a better community. Their work ethic is equal or sur-passes that of many of our native born. And that's how we have dealt with the challenge. We'd like to see more new Americans settled in Concord and in the state."

Population growth can potentially come to the state from three sources: births minus deaths (natural increase), domestic migration of people from other states, and international migration (immigration) from other nations. From 2010 to 2018, the number of people living year-round in New Hampshire increased by about 40,800. That total included about 9,100 more births than deaths, and a net gain of about 6,800 people who moved here from other states. The balance of 24,900 individuals came to New Hampshire from other countries.

Immigration has accounted for 61% of New Hampshire's population growth since 2010. Few people have noticed over this past decade that more than three times as many people came here from other countries as moved here from other states.

"The population decline and dramatic aging taking place in cities and towns across northern New England have real, long-term consequences," advises a Federal Reserve Bank of Boston policy brief published in July 2019. "Northern New England, even more so than the rest of the country, depends increasingly on immigration to sustain population growth in the face of a declining birth rate." The complete report, "Aging and Declining Populations in Northern New England: Is There a Role for Immigration?" is authored by Riley Sullivan of the Boston Fed's New England Public Policy Center and available at www.bostonfed.org.

The Boston Fed's town-level analysis shows that immigrants who have moved to Maine, New Hampshire, and Vermont since 1990 have not settled just in the "larger, younger, and thriving communities; they also have settled in smaller towns and contributed to the growth of the population in those municipalities."

Some immigration occurred in all 10 New Hampshire counties, but about half of new Americans arriving since 2010 settled in Hillsborough County. Four other counties—Merrimack, Rockingham, Strafford, and Grafton—each received more than 2,000 immigrants since 2010. In all five counties, one or more major employers are recruiting employees globally.

The greatest cause of population change in New England since the 1990s is declining natural increase—births minus deaths. Birth rates have fallen while mortality rates are rising, due to the increased numbers of older residents. Declining birth rates not only slow overall population growth, but also contribute to an even faster rate of aging—of an already relatively old population.

Immigration is playing a growing role in sustaining many communities across the region. "In New England, immigration is sustaining communities and the nonwhite population is growing," wrote Carla Koppell in the September 17, 2019, New England Journal of Higher Education. "New arrivals are bolstering the labor force, driving entrepreneurship and innovation, and providing different skills than native-born residents. They are also compensating for decreases in the locally born population, helping to maintain communities that would otherwise wither. The heterogeneity of people and perspectives is increasingly visible too; social media and information technology accelerate the flow of information crossing communities."

Population aging and population decline are two distinct demographic phenomena, each carrying its own range of implications for communities, the Boston Fed brief notes. A declining local population "depletes the available workforce, diminishes the tax base, weakens the health of the business environment and the housing market, and destabilizes institutions such as schools and hospitals." In addition to similarly negative workforce and tax-base consequences, an aging population also poses unique demands on public services.

Loss of working-age residents, ages 18 to 64, has direct and indirect, short- and long-term consequences for a community's workforce and tax base. "In the short term, it results in smaller per capita output. In the longer run, when prime-age residents leave a community, they take their children and their reproductive potential with them, exacerbating the negative effect of their out-migration on the population size and age structure," the Boston Fed brief explains. "Because of this generational effect, net out-migration of young adults contributes to a cumulative process of population decline and aging."

Declining numbers of working-age residents can result in employers deciding to expand or outright move their businesses elsewhere. Thus begins a downward spiral of stagnant or declining local tax revenue to spend on infrastructure and education. "An inferior infrastructure and school system, in turn, can encourage the younger people who had remained in the region to head elsewhere for more opportunity. This can cascade into further problems by making the region a less attractive destination for migration..."

Likely outcomes, the Boston Fed brief warns, include decreases in the number of establishments providing financial services, education, and leisure and hospitality activities. "Declining student enrollment, resulting from a decrease in the size of the school-age population, can deprive schools of resources and make it difficult to remain open." Increasing median age also leads to decreasing resident access to services, even when population is not in decline.

Although comprising less than five percent of northern New England's overall population as of 2017, immigrants have made substantial contributions to the region's population growth in recent years. Between 1990 and 2017, the three northern New England states together added nearly 60,000 immigrants—a growth rate of 63%— while the size of the native-born population increased by less than 12%. In seven of the 10 years from 2009 through 2018, the population of New England would have shrunk or failed to grow without the influx of new Americans.

"If the flow of immigration is reduced or limited, which seems to be the trajectory of current national policy, the demographic vise that is squeezing rural towns across northern New England will become even tighter, and policymakers will have limited options for responding," the Boston Fed brief cautions. "As natural increase continues to decline, immigration is expected to become the primary contributor to national population growth after 2030."

A 2018 Census Bureau survey found that people who have come to New Hampshire from other countries—new Americans—have similar characteristics to those who were already here. The survey of 21,000 New Hampshire residents who had entered the country since 2010 found that 27% had bachelor's degrees, 28% held graduate degrees, and 42% were employed in management, business or scientific occupations. Those percentages are not materially different from the education and professional profiles of US-born residents. Steve Duprey of The Duprey Companies characterizes new immigrants as "New Americans—who as employees are indistinguishable from all the other people who work here."

While half our counties are experiencing net out-migration of residents who leave for other states, every one of our 10 counties benefits from some immigration. New Americans settling in the Granite State have come from every continent, and they are helping to enrich the culture and life of our communities. They and their families are seeking the same American dream as those born here. New Americans are putting down roots and weaving diversity and resilience into the fabric of our communities, large and small, all across our state.

Unlocking Heritage and Growth in Lancaster

3

In Coos County, the northernmost and second-grayest in the state, things are looking up in Lancaster. The county's second-largest municipality throws more weight than its population of 3,300 would suggest. Located astride the intersection of US routes 2 and 3, Lancaster is the county seat and commercial and cultural center for the region. Like other aging manufacturing towns, population and businesses had dwindled over time. But these days abandoned, dilapidated, and under-utilized downtown buildings are being restored and repurposed, one after another.

Lancaster's increasingly lively downtown offers inviting places to eat, including the Polish Princess Bakery, the Granite Grind farm-to-table café, a popular local brew-pub and a Caribbean-Jamaican restaurant. The restored historic movie theater shows current films. Popular with locals and tourists alike, the Lancaster Farmers Market meets at Centennial Park along Main Street every Saturday morning in season, with live music and more than 30 vendors. Modern apartments created on the second and third floors of commercial buildings are just what many young professionals, singles, and couples of all life cycle stages are seeking. Both the town's preschool-8 elementary school and the regional high school have been named New Hampshire Schools of Excellence.

The secret ingredients to Lancaster's transformative downtown successes and rekindled civic pride involve historic preservation, openness to change, and something called "form-based code." This technical term for a new approach to zoning and building regulations sounds like arcane planning jargon—but it's a practical, common-sense approach that lets people shape the future of their community.

Ben Gaetjens-Oleson, a Lancaster native now in his 40s, has served as town planning and zoning coordinator since 2009. Oleson was a featured speaker at the 2019 New Hampshire Preservation Alliance Conference held in Littleton, a North Country town with a famously revitalized downtown. He presented a seminar on how Lancaster changed course through historic preservation and form-based code. Through the 1980s and 1990s, Lancaster had experienced an all-too-familiar cycle of demolition of older houses and businesses to make way for a series of fast-food and gas station/convenience store developments, as well as a supermarket.

"In 1995, a Rite-Aid replaced a beautiful creamery building and an older home," Oleson told the preservation conference attendees. "The town did nothing to prevent or discourage this kind of development. The zoning said this is commercial use, and this is what you can do." Amendments to zoning and site plan review regulations failed to resolve the conflicts between older buildings and new development.

"If a proposed development met minimum requirements," Oleson said, "it got approved." A series of events began to change people's outlooks. Fires had burned out several older buildings in the downtown, leaving scarred vacant lots. In 2011, a Family Dollar store was proposed and built right next to the Rite-Aid, requiring the demolition of two more old houses. The town's approaching 250th anniversary celebration in 2014 was turning residents' attention to their town's heritage, to the community assets that had been lost, and those remaining in peril.

■ Turning Point

The town wanted a different kind of development. The master plan completed in 2011 set broad goals of maintaining or improving quality of life, sense of community, the rural and unique character and economic footing of the town, and preservation of the historic character and resources of Main Street. The master plan spelled out what the town wanted its village center to look like, including specifics such as preference for side or rear parking. Residents said in their master plan that they valued and wanted to preserve the dramatic, open vistas of agricultural lands and forested mountains from all major roads leading into town. Increasing the quantity and quality of housing for people of all ages, incomes, and family sizes was a priority, while also minimizing the consumption of land.

Recognizing that existing zoning and building regulations did not align with the desired master plan outcomes, in 2013 the town engaged planning consultants Steve Whitman and the late Jeff Taylor to undertake a thorough audit of how the town's zoning and building regulations matched up with the goals and directions in the master plan.

The audit identified critical areas where the town's regulations were in direct conflict with what the community said it wanted in the master plan. What the people of Lancaster wanted to see in their downtown would require a dramatically different approach to zoning, Oleson says. In 2014, the town voted for that change by adopting the proposed downtown form-based code by an overwhelming two-to-one vote.

That strong support grew through an extensive public input-gathering process, including four public meetings, a

Saturday charrette facilitated by the planning consultants, and specific outreach to high-school students and the elder members of the community.

As Steve Whitman, now of Resilience Planning & Design LLC, explains in an article about Lancaster on his firm's website:

> A form-based code addresses the relationship between buildings and the public realm (streets, sidewalks, etc.), and the form and mass of buildings in relation to one another... The regulations and standards in Lancaster's form-based code are presented using words and clearly drawn diagrams, and really call for a pattern of design and development that is similar to what exists in the downtown today.

Lancaster created form-based codes tailored to the three distinct sections of its Main Street. The section with the roundabout is more car-centric, for example. Oleson says that adopting RSA 79-E Community Revitalization Tax Incentive (see Appendix: Resource Toolkit) was also important in making some of the building restorations and improvements financially feasible. Another key factor is people who are able and motivated to invest in the community. A number of businesses, non-profit organizations, and property owners have made significant investments in improving the downtown buildings and properties. Greg Cloutier, a Lancaster resident and businessman, has undertaken a series of major projects. Cloutier, in turn, says the town has stepped up, too, such as financing the digital projector for the restored Rialto movie theater.

■ Investing in Community

At 70, Cloutier says his career in industrial engineering and hydropower left him in a financial position where he can choose to put his money to work locally. Having grown up in nearby

View of Lancaster's revitalizing downtown, with the restored historic Rialto Theater in the foreground.

Groveton, Cloutier returned to the area after college, in an era when industry was thriving.

Cloutier's first downtown project earned recognition from the New Hampshire Preservation Alliance with a 2015 Preservation Achievement Award for the rescue of two prominent buildings at 73–77 Main Street in Lancaster and the resulting contributions to revitalizing the social and economic fabric of the downtown.

Cloutier agrees that restoring what had been a burned-out eyesore has had real impact on the downtown. But it's not just the building, he says, it's the people in the building. This project gave two new local food entrepreneurs space to grow their visions. Magda Randall has seen her Polish Princess Bakery thrive and gain statewide attention. Melissa Greller, founder of the nonprofit Taproot Farm and Environmental Education Center, was able to establish the Root Seller Marketplace food

> "It's the residential units that make the whole thing work. There are people downtown, coming and going. The activity attracts more people. It gets businesses interested in being here."
>
> —Greg Cloutier, Lancaster businessman and preservationist

hub and local and natural food store. The Root Seller has rapidly outgrown the space. Cloutier has reserved prime space for a larger Root Seller Market in the plans for his next building restoration.

"Anybody can build a building," Cloutier advises. "It's having the right people in the building." If he were to own up to having a talent for downtown development, it would be in spotting entrepreneurial potential in people motivated to serve and benefit their community. He is proud of the new businesses that have filled his and other buildings downtown and the "new blood" they have brought to the community.

The new form-based code made it possible for Cloutier to take on renovation and creative reuse of the former Lancaster National Bank building that dominates one end of Main Street. It's now a business center with the Copper Pig Brewery and Pub in the basement where guests enter through the bank vault doors, a fine art gallery, and other local shops and businesses. Cloutier says restrictions in the old zoning—like excessive parking requirements—made apartments prohibitively expensive to build. The specifications of the new form-based code, such as dimensions and building heights, are what he would choose to build.

Cloutier's next project—preservation, rehabilitation and multi-use redevelopment of the Parker J. Noyes Building— is a joint venture with the Northern Forest Center, a regional innovation and investment partner dedicated to creating vibrant communities by connecting people and the economy to the forested landscape. Cloutier says Northern Forest Center is an "entrepreneurial, enterprising nonprofit," and the cost of bringing back this building just would not be feasible without grant funding. A nonprofit partner provides access to grants and other assistance.

The Noyes Building, selected in 2017 for the NH Preservation Alliance's Seven to Save list, has an interesting story. Thanks to Parker J. Noyes, Lancaster became a flourishing center of pharmaceutical manufacturing. Noyes was a pharmacist and inventor of innovations including the sugar-coated pill and the first precision food pellet for laboratory animals. For a time, this building was the largest pharmaceutical products manufacturing facility in the United States. It has anchored the northern downtown since 1846. In the 1960s, the Parker J. Noyes Company left Main Street for a new plant on the outskirts of town, where its corporate successor continues to operate.

By the twenty-first century, the Parker J. Noyes Building was in sore need of rehabilitation and a plan, which got it on the Seven to Save list. "This imposing Italianate block forms the northern gateway into the village, its future is critical to the health of Lancaster," reads the NH Preservation Alliance's citation.

The first floor of the Noyes Building will become the new home of the Taproot Farm and Environmental Education Center, which will move its Root Seller Marketplace from Cloutier's first Main Street building. The Root Seller provides year-round access to fresh, local food and serves as a food hub connecting farmers and food producers with buyers and consumers throughout the region. Expansion plans include a commercial kitchen for the Root Seller. Taproot, founded by Melissa Greller, also manages the Lancaster Community Garden and the NH North Country Gleaners, which gathers locally produced foods for food pantries, plus several environmental education programs. The two upper floors will be turned into six two-bedroom apartments for young professionals and families who want to enjoy downtown living.

The Northern Forest Center and Cloutier have heard from a community advisory group, as well as market conditions, of the need for more high-quality commercial and residential building space to house young families and professionals. Cloutier notes that not just young people, but some empty-nesters and older residents may also prefer walkable downtown living. The Noyes Building will add to the two-to-three dozen apartments that Oleson estimates currently exist downtown. These units have proven popular and are typically fully rented. The local hospital leases some of the apartments for traveling medical staff— doctors, nurses, and technicians.

The Northern Forest Center sees potential in the Parker J. Noyes Building to radically transform Lancaster's downtown. The Center has raised private investments to fund the purchase and renovation of the building, attracting investors who want to put their money to work doing good things for the community while also earning a financial return. "Our investors want their money to leverage new energy and vibrancy in Lancaster's downtown," Center President Rob Riley has stated. "We've seen how quality redevelopment of important buildings can help communities turn a corner and how one project quickly leads to other enhancements."

Form-based Codes Defined

A form-based code is a land-development regulation that fosters predictable built results and a high-quality public realm by using physical form (rather than separation of uses) as the organizing principle for the code. A form-based code is a regulation, not a mere guideline, adopted into city, town, or county law. A form-based code offers a powerful alternative to conventional zoning regulation.

Form-based codes address the relationship between building facades and the public realm, the form and mass of buildings in relation to one another, and the scale and types of streets and blocks. The regulations and standards in form-based codes are presented in both words and clearly drawn diagrams and other visuals. They are keyed to a regulating plan that designates the appropriate form and scale (and therefore, character) of development, rather than only distinctions in land-use types.

This approach contrasts with conventional zoning's focus on the micromanagement and segregation of land uses, and the control of development intensity through abstract and uncoordinated parameters (FAR, dwellings per acre, setbacks, parking ratios, traffic LOS) to the neglect of an integrated built form. Not to be confused with design guidelines or general statements of policy, form-based codes are regulatory, not advisory. They are drafted to implement a community plan. They try to achieve a community vision based on time-tested forms of urbanism. Ultimately, a form-based code is a tool; the quality of development outcomes depends on the quality and objectives of the community plan that a code implements.

What Makes a Good Form-based Code?

Putting together a high-quality public realm is not easy. Public and private spaces need to be arranged in a way that enlivens the street and creates a memorable place. This means careful placement and orientation of buildings, engaging building design, and common-sense parking standards that add up to an inviting public space for pedestrians. Close coordination and cooperation with the departments of public works and emergency services on street standards and designs that fit their surroundings is also important.

Conventional, use-based zoning codes are often heavy on text, short on illustrations, and use overly technical language. Good form-based codes are designed to make zoning approachable, concise, and understandable for everyone—a first-time homeowner, a developer, an architect, or a skilled planning professional. The layout should make navigating the document easy, and the outcome and steps in the decision-making tree and the development outcome should be clearly defined. All technical terms are spelled out in plain English, and graphics and images are plentiful to convey the intent—a picture is worth a thousand words, especially when talking about form.

Exemplary form-based codes successfully create walkable and identifiable neighborhoods that provide most of life's daily needs in close proximity to places where people live, work, and play.

Form-based zoning harkens back to the land-use practices of the past that focused on building walkable, interesting communities for people, as opposed to conventional zoning, which has segregated people and encouraged destructive sprawl. As communities across the country seek to manage growth in a sustainable, equitable way—i.e. smart growth—they are turning to form-based codes to provide the regulatory framework for such growth.

Source: Form-Based Codes Institute
1152 15th Street NW, Ste. 450, Washington DC 20005
202-868-4103
https://formbasedcodes.org

Cloutier is glad to provide space for the Root Seller Market to grow, as the Root Seller expands markets for local farmers and producers. Nothing makes Cloutier happier than to see businesses thriving in the buildings he has rehabilitated and developed—and all the growth in downtown activity.

"It's the residential units that make the whole thing work," Cloutier emphasizes. "There are people downtown, coming and going. The activity attracts more people. It gets businesses interested in being here."

■ Young Professionals Liking What They Find

More people do seem to be choosing to make their homes and careers here. Particularly people who work at the hospital and the schools, notes Oleson. People like Jacob and Blair Hess, a pair of young educators born and raised in upstate New York, who found their way to jobs at White Mountains Regional High School, the five-town district high school located nearby in Whitefield.

Blair Hess, 26, is a school guidance counselor who grew up in East Syracuse, New York, but always wanted to be in New England. She applied for jobs in four New England states. Her first interview was at White Mountains Regional, and it was love at first sight. "I had researched it, and I loved the school!" she says. She was impressed by the equity and quality of the career and technical education programs—and by "the incredible view, right from campus!" She immediately wanted to live here, she says.

Her English teacher husband, Jacob, 35, liked the idea of teaching at a smaller school. Coming from a school with 17 English teachers, 1,600 students and more than 200 faculty, he says White Mountains Regional's four English teachers and 360 students sounded like a friendlier atmosphere that provided "more chance for me to make a difference." He was right about that. In his second year, he was promoted to chair of the English department, and the next year he was tapped as assistant principal.

The Hesses rented in Littleton their first year, where they enjoyed the lively downtown, but not the commute to work and daycare for their then two-year-old daughter. They set their sights on Lancaster. "It's close to work, has the kids' programs, and is a great school district," Blair noted, also checking off in-town amenities including a movie theater, parks, and restaurants. A couple of friends from work had also bought a house in Lancaster and were planning to start a family.

"Nothing could beat Lancaster" as a place, Blair Hess says, but finding a house was not so easy. Houses were either cheap and in poor condition, or too much money for their budget, limited by their graduate-school debt. They rented for two years before finally finding a house they liked and could afford. Unlike the area of central New York that they left, they found no new houses or neighborhoods here. But the Hesses are very happy with the solid, well-built, and updated 130-year-old home they now own.

Two new teachers at the high school, both single women, have also recently chosen to live in Lancaster—one purchased a house, and the other is renting a downtown apartment. The Hesses say that school staff members take new hires under their wings to help them feel at home in the North Country community. "For some people it is kind of a culture shock," Blair Hess says.

"Retention of staff has improved drastically over the last several years," Jacob Hess observes. "More are staying, and we're getting higher quality applicants. It's really been a great move for us."

■ Retaining and Attracting Young People

A crucial question for the future of Lancaster and the whole region is how many of today's students will choose to stay or return to the area to work, start businesses, and raise families. A decade-long study of Coos County youth by the University of New Hampshire

Carsey School of Public Policy looked at what influences the decisions young people make to leave the region or to stay, and what draws back those who return. "The sense of community among Coos youth is strong and remained resilient in the face of the Great Recession," the study concluded. "The exception is youth voice, which remained low in comparison to school belonging, community integration, and community support."

"Youth who feel like their voices are heard during childhood and adolescence may be more prone to desire a long-term future in Coos even if they leave for a while during early adulthood to pursue educational or professional opportunities elsewhere," concluded researcher Cesar Rebellon. (Get the full report at https://carsey.unh.edu/new-hampshire.)

Ben Oleson, Lancaster's town planner, has made a point of including youth voices in the downtown planning process and has established positions for two high-school student representatives on the planning board. "Including the youth of Lancaster and the immediate area in the planning process is a deliberate effort to bring a different perspective to community development," Oleson explains. "An additional intent is to hopefully get a greater interest and investment from this underutilized demographic that will result in more of our kids remaining in, or returning to, the area to start careers and families."

Andy Smith, a 2019 graduate of White Mountains Regional High School and one of the student representatives to the planning board, chose to focus his senior capstone project on the economic benefits and history of the Lancaster Fair. Reflecting the town's agricultural past and present, the Lancaster Fair draws tens of thousands every Labor Day weekend to the sprawling 65-acre fairgrounds along Route 3.

Smith surveyed community members and businesses that participated in the fair. "I was able to conclude that many people from all age groups like having the fair," he notes. All businesses that participated in his survey reported that the fair was good for business. Smith's capstone presentation also focused on the fair's long history and how it has evolved over nearly a century and a half.

"With my research I found that there was a lot more to Lancaster than I thought," Smith, who was heading to Keene State College to study secondary education and history, wrote in an email. "Which made me consider the idea of possibly staying in the area after college. However, many of my peers intend on moving away and leaving the area."

"We're slowly creating an environment that young people like—but that local people also appreciate," Oleson says of Lancaster's revitalization.

Greg Cloutier agrees. "Something's happening here," he observes with palpable pride in the town. "People are friendly."

New Hampshire Communities Using Form-based Code

In December 2009, the city of Dover became the first New Hampshire community to adopt a form-based code for its downtown. Dover's new downtown investment and growth in youthful entrepreneurship have sparked envy in other towns and cities.

"A guiding principal behind the development of a form-based code is that the buildings and physical alteration of land is more long-lasting than the initial use found within the building that is constructed, and we should be concerned about community character and appearance," explains an article about Dover's downtown form-based code on the city's website.

The state's Office of Strategic Initiatives reports that in 2018 six communities—Dover, Enfield, Lancaster,

Milford, Portsmouth, and Stratham—"have gone a step further and created form-based codes for some or all of their community, which regulate the character and physical form of an area rather than specific uses."

Steve Whitman and the late Jeff Taylor, then working together as Jeffrey Taylor & Associates, facilitated Dover's process, holding a series of community-design charrettes and even physically measuring buildings identified by residents as examples of what they wanted to preserve and emulate.

Whitman, now of Resilience Planning & Design LLC in Plymouth, reports he is getting more calls from communities looking, like Lancaster and Dover, for more lively spaces around the stay-work-play theme. The non-profit organization by that name—Stay Work Play New Hampshire—has helped raise awareness of the demographic imbalance of the state and of the many opportunities and features of our state that are valued by younger workers and professionals.

Whitman says many communities are focused on reinforcing—or in some cases creating—downtowns with mixed-use development so people can live in walkable communities, close to where they work, socialize, and recreate. "It's gotten to the point where housing affordability is at the forefront," Whitman says. More communities are working to have more diversity of housing choices for different ages, incomes, and life-cycle stages. Housing close to jobs can mean real cost-of-living benefits, by reducing or eliminating commuting time and expense. Many also connect these changes to sustainability, reduced environmental impacts, and renewal of natural resources.

Stratham is an example of a community seeking to create an area of pedestrian-friendly, mixed-use development that residents have felt the community lacked. In

March 2010, the Seacoast town became the second community in the state to adopt a form-based code zoning ordinance—for its new Gateway Business Commercial District.

Stratham's form-based code aims over time to convert an area dominated by unappealing commercial strip-development to the Gateway Commercial Business District vision of enhancing "the economic vitality, business diversity, accessibility, and visual appeal of Stratham's built environment, in a manner that is consistent with the landscape and architecture of the Town's agricultural tradition." Achieving these changes requires development of sewer and water service to the district in order to support the desired density and diversity of occupants—such as restaurants or cafes, and apartments over commercial and office spaces. Convincing residents to support adding these services with a bond issue is challenging but essential to achieving the vision the town has agreed upon.

When the 2018 Stratham Town Report was published, Select Board Vice Chair Joe Lovejoy observed with chagrin that yet again, the town had recorded more deaths than births—more than three times as many. And this is a prosperous Seacoast town known for good schools and as a good place to raise a family. Just a generation ago, the numbers were reversed, with three births for every death. "We've been headed in the direction of making ourselves extinct," Lovejoy declared. He's hoping the Gateway District provisions and new master plan will get the town headed "on the right road."

This statement, or warning, in Stratham's draft 2019 master plan could apply to many, if not most, towns in southern New Hampshire:

"The path on which this community is traveling is one where the housing market gradually consumes our available land, including our farmland, and makes it possible only for the wealthy to live here. If no changes are made to current land use policies and the community does not invest in a different future, the Community Vision articulated in this Master Plan will not be achieved."

The capital city of Concord completed a major facelift with redesigned traffic patterns and parking in its historic downtown in 2015. The downtown and capital district are now more inviting and hospitable to pedestrians and cyclists. Soon thereafter, the city's planning department tackled the complex challenges of improving the livability and diversity of the whole city. In 2018, the city launched Concord NEXT, an ambitious two-year effort to rethink zoning across the city, neighborhood by neighborhood. Guided by the Concord 20/20 Vision of a "city of villages set in an extraordinary natural landscape," the city hired Code Studio planning consultants of Austin, Texas, to lead development of form-based code zoning for the entire city.

The Concord planning department website has a wealth of information about this work in progress and explains that the "new illustrated document will present a guide to 'character-based' development that focuses on the physical form and character of the neighborhood that the community wants to create or preserve."

Objectives include creating new standards that will "enhance and expand the walkable, livable urban fabric of the City. Enhance amenities for existing residents. Attract a new population of young professionals and families." City planners say the new approach to zoning will greatly reduce the need for variances in this older city, where non-conforming properties are the rule rather than the exception and often represent what people like most about the city. Form-based code aims to do just that—regulate the appearance, scale, and proportions of a community, rather than focusing on the uses of the built environment.

City Planner Heather Shank was hired in 2015. She says this major undertaking grew from plans for community visioning and revitalization of the village of Penacook. The city's Community Development Advisory Committee had a strong interest in form-based code for Penacook. "We began asking—do we just want to do Penacook," Shank says, "—or do we want to do a whole update of the zoning code?" The whole zoning document needed cleaning up, she allows, since the existing 2001 zoning did not reflect either "what we had, or what we wanted."

The old zoning for the long stretch of the city dubbed the "opportunity corridor"— from New Hampshire Technical College down I-93 and the Merrimack River to South Concord—plus the commercial sprawl of Loudon Road was all single-use districts; "What we don't want," Shank stresses. Today's failed or declining shopping malls are prime examples of development regulated for a specific single use.

The form-based codes drafted for the first phase—mostly in-town neighborhoods—directly address the lack of housing diversity. "We have very few attached houses, for example," Shank says. The new code would allow and promote different housing types. It also would allow "a lot more flexibility on properties." Residents were asked what they thought they should be able to do on their properties—and what they should not be able to do. The emphasis will be on the visual character of neighborhoods—size of lots, how much building on lots, and equity in housing. "If you have sufficient land," Shank explains, "you can have two units in a house."

"Form-based code is just a zoning tool," Shank says, "—a different way of writing information, relying more on graphics." She believes it is a "better way to communicate the information." She explains to the many groups she speaks to around the city that "form-based code makes it easier for people to make their community the way they want." For Concord, that goal will continue to be a "city of villages" that values preserving its open, natural spaces.

Growing Your Own: New Generation Revitalizes Bradford

4

A sign on the road coming into the town of Bradford pro-claims: "Gateway to the Sunapee Region."

"As if this is just a place on the way to somewhere else," Hanna Flanders remarks in response.

The 30-year-old is one of five founding members of the Kearsarge Food Hub and among the growing network of young people settling in this rural small-town area of New Hampshire where most of them grew up.

It all started, Flanders explains, with shared goals of ramping up opportunities for local farm and food enterprises, and helping to create a vibrant community for residents of

What Is a "Food Hub"?

According to the US Department of Agriculture's *Regional Food Hub Resource Guide*, a food hub is a "business or organization that actively manages the aggregation, distribution, and marketing of course-identified food products primarily from local and regional producers to strengthen their ability to satisfy wholesale, retail, and institutional demand."

all ages and backgrounds. First came Sweet Beet Farm. They harvested their first vegetables in 2015 and have been growing ever since. That's become their slogan—*"Grow with us."* Now colorful, hand-lettered signs with arrows direct people to the 'Sweet Beet Market' in the restored historic Bradford Inn on West Main Street. Everyone in town seems to refer to the food hub movers and shakers as "the Sweet Beets."

Bradford is about 30 miles northwest of Concord and seven miles south of I-89 off Exit 9. The 2010 US Census calculated Bradford's median age at 46.1 years—about five years older than even the Merrimack County or state medians. While the town grew at a little faster rate than the state as a whole from 2000 to 2010, Bradford had lost population and businesses over the decades before. Shuttered, vacant businesses and large rundown buildings bore testament to the community's more prosperous past as a tourist destination. The estimated 2017 population was 1,685. Median household income is $67,857, compared to the state median $73,381.

After graduating from Kearsarge Regional High School, Flanders and the friends who would eventually return to rejuvenate Bradford went off to different colleges, both in and out of

Kearsarge Food Hub: Who We Are

We are a nonprofit organization seeking well-being and connection for all through community service. Our objectives include promoting community cohesion, increasing access to local food, and contributing to the economic and environmental viability of our area.

We are community supporters. We are farmer advocates. We are stewards of the land.

—From the Kearsarge Food Hub website,
www.kearsargefoodhub.org

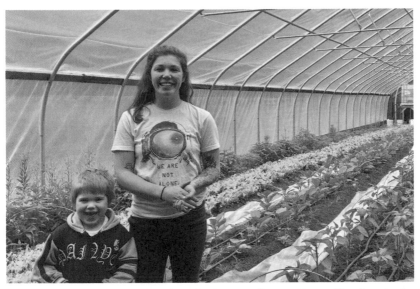

Sweet Beet communications and marketing coordinator, Hanna Flanders, in the Sweet Beet Farm high-tunnel greenhouse with her five-year-old son, Chase.

state. From college, they dispersed to other parts of the country or the wider world, but their love for the beauty and nature of this rural part of central New Hampshire and the tug of family and community roots was strong.

In 2015, Flanders and four friends—then in their mid-20s—founded the Kearsarge Food Hub, a nonprofit organization that has spawned an expanding network of farm and food enterprises and much more. Flanders studied philosophy and environmental science and policy at Smith College. Sister and brother France and Pierre Hahn, born in France but raised in Bradford, consider it their hometown. Pierre went to Syracuse University, and France studied at McGill University in Montreal. At McGill, she befriended Lauren Howard from Kennebunk, Maine, who became the sole founding member from "away." Bradford native Garrett Bauer, the fifth founding member, studied eco-gastronomy at UNH and gleaned a lot from the program's study-abroad experience in Italy.

■ Sweet Beet Generation Connects Food, Community, Family, Education, Nature

Flanders says some founding members had farming experience, but all had witnessed habitat destruction in their travels, and all saw a need to strengthen the local farming economy. "We all saw food as the link connecting the values of community, family, education, and nature, and to the generations before. We're inheriting wisdom from those who came before us," Flanders says. This group of young people actively seeks, and has benefitted from advice, support, and partnerships with people in the community of other generations.

Kearsarge Food Hub began with two small farming plots in town—patches of land owned by a community member and by the Hahn siblings. They sold their produce from a small, seasonal roadside farm stand and at farmers markets. They also marketed some produce from other farms in the area. As the farming enterprise took root and grew, they needed a year-round, larger outlet.

■ Private Initiatives Accelerate Sweat Equity

During this same period, a slightly older couple had moved to Bradford when they fell in love with the old farmhouse they now call home. Mike James, 41, says he and his wife Claire were able to leave New Jersey because of the flexibility of his work in IT consulting and software. The Jameses liked the idea of living in a small town and wanted to get involved. "It's easier to make a difference," he says. He attended a town revitalization meeting, where someone suggested that private initiatives were important. "I took that to heart," he says.

The first project Mike James tackled was converting an old, derelict lot in town into an ecologically designed permaculture garden filled with native and food-producing plants.

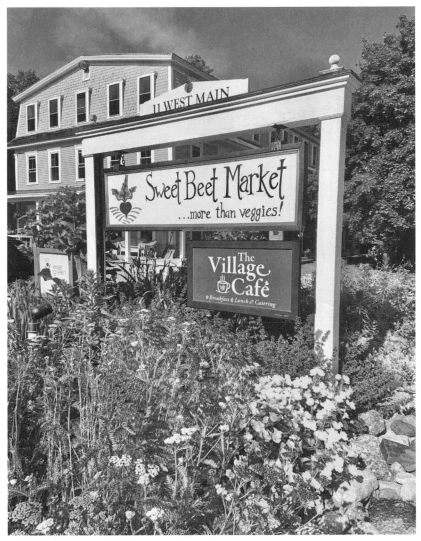

The restored historic Bradford Inn is now home to the Sweet Beet Market, the Village Café, a yoga studio, and other new businesses.

Long-time resident Mike Bauer—who happens to be Garrett Bauer's father—started helping out, and others pitched in, too. Soon a new gardening club formed, and it has since taken on continuing care of the garden.

Mike James says he was always mindful of the importance of health and wellness—but until getting involved in Bradford, he had not recognized the crucial role of community in the health of people and the environment. He and new friend Mike Bauer found themselves eyeing the historic Bradford Inn building, which was falling apart on West Main Street in the center of town. "There was this group of kids who had come back to the town," James says of the Kearsarge Food Hub group, who needed a bigger space to expand their Sweet Beet Market. "Other young people had also been attracted here—we thought maybe other businesses could work in the inn, too."

The two Mikes bought the old inn building and began rehabilitating it floor by floor. In 2018, the Sweet Beet Market became their first tenant. Soon after, two local women, who were originally from England and had run a small catering business in town, opened the Village Café in adjoining space on the first floor of the restored inn building. They use the food hub's commercial kitchen and serve baked goods made by Sweet Beet baker Garrett Bauer.

Customers enter Sweet Beet Market and the Village Café from the wide, welcoming porch of the historic inn building. Large windows and high ceilings create a bright and airy space for displaying fresh and processed foods from the Sweet Beet Farm and from more than 30 producers within a 30-mile radius. In their first year, the market and café were fast becoming a favorite stop for people from Bradford and communities well beyond.

In such a small town, Flanders says, when the only food store had closed some years before, the community was left without a public gathering place where people exchanged news and kept up connections through busy daily lives. "We're seeing our Sweet Beet Market starting to fill that role now," she says with pride.

A yoga studio was added on the second floor of the restored historic building. Other businesses finding room at the inn include a start-up that helps health-care institutions with their recycling needs. Hanna Flanders's husband Jon is co-owner, and Jon's business partner and his wife also grew up in Bradford.

"With the internet and technology today, you can create your own jobs," Flanders declares. She and Jon have two young children, and they are grateful to be raising their young family in a community and environment they love. Aspiring to buy a home and send their children to school in the same district they attended, for now student debt keeps them in a rented apartment in a neighboring town.

This group of young people is most appreciative of the support they have received from members of the Bradford community and others in the region, including the Warner Public Market. Two more members have officially joined the Food Hub group. Bea Ross, also 30 and a Kearsarge High School graduate, earned her degree from Plymouth State University and volunteered with AmeriCorps as a recycling educator and coordinator in Tennessee. Back in Bradford, she now manages Sweet Beet Market.

Flanders says that recognizing a "need for some balance," the group enticed Kathleen Bigford, a retired schoolteacher with strong interests in food systems and community, to join the food hub. Her younger colleagues joke about her being their den mother, but Flanders says Bigford, age 70, plays "an essential role."

Part of the 1970s back-to-the-land movement, Bigford and her husband moved to Bradford from Washington, DC, as young adults in 1974. Seeking to live and raise a family in a rural area, she started an organic garden, helped organize a local food-buying co-op, and enjoyed being able to cross-country ski from right out their back door. Over the intervening years, she became busy with her middle-school teaching career, raising their daughter, and community life. By the time she retired in 2015, she was already busy teaching gardening in after-school programs in a neighboring district. Then France and Pierre Hahn approached her about joining the food hub.

■ "If this had been going on when I was getting ready to leave..."

The Bigfords' only daughter is now married and lives and works in Colorado. "She has told us several times," Bigford says wistfully, "that 'if this [the food hub activity] had been going on when I was getting ready to leave, I would have stayed. But nothing was happening here then.'"

But today's up-and-coming generations are benefiting and participating. Bigford is deeply involved in the food hub's education work, from early childhood to college levels. Colby Sawyer College students participate in hands-on farming experience and research projects, and environmental sciences professor Leon Malan serves on the food hub board. Bigford says the Sweet Beet farms give opportunities to high-school students from Kearsarge Regional High School and from John Stark Regional High School's Equity Program "to put down their phones and get to work." Bradford Elementary first- and second-graders all participate in a series of seasonal hands-on activities provided both at school and at the farm—like harvesting potatoes and onions.

■ Younger People Join Town Boards

With the garden project and saving the inn, Mike and Claire James grew so committed to their new hometown and to growing all these new community connections that they both ran and were elected to local office—she is on the planning board and he is a selectman. In his second year, James was elected chair of the select board. The following year a second new member, Jason Allen, was elected to the three-person board. "He's younger than me," Mike James notes. "He's excited about parks and recreation—and walking trails."

The select board wants to complete a network of trails connecting to businesses and town facilities to build community and support local businesses. The last master plan, adopted in 2006, put priorities on creating trail systems, but not much had happened. The town's young leaders see trails as a benefit to all ages in town, noting that the senior activities coordinator is excited that the plan will tie the community center, where senior activities are held, to the trail network.

"I'm really, really positive about Bradford," Mike James enthuses. "There's getting to be a lot of young families." But much work remains. The select board wants to create a vision aligned with the updated master plan. James says he "didn't bring these ideas from New Jersey!" It's the people of Bradford, he says, who have shown him the meaning and value of community.

■ A Bridge to Cross: Housing

As elsewhere in the state, housing is a major need—more diverse types and sizes of homes in good condition and affordable at varying incomes and life-cycle stages are still scarce. "Communities should support multi-generational families," Mike James asserts. Seniors should be able to stay in town, if they choose, and younger generations should be able to live and raise their families there as well. More apartments or cottage-size homes are needed.

"Finding a decent, affordable place to rent is definitely a challenge in our area," Hanna Flanders reports, "and in Bradford specifically." Tourism in the Lake Sunapee region results in very expensive seasonal rentals. "But affordable, clean and well-maintained year-round rentals are lacking," she adds. Anything for sale in a reasonable price range needs a lot of work. She says some members of their younger group "definitely struggle to find affordable housing, especially since we are still working on making our nonprofit financially viable and in a position to pay truly living wages." And several young community members need to pay down significant student loan debt before they can qualify for a mortgage.

Flanders sees a combination of factors preventing construction of affordable housing suitable for younger or older community members. "We have an interesting demographic where we have seasonal visitors with a lot more money, and then we have year-round residents needing affordable houses," she says. "I imagine it is much more lucrative for builders to build for folks who have a lot of money, and probably not a lot of incentives from the town to do otherwise. I have also heard that there are many hurdles to building in terms of regulations."

Several of her friends have looked into alternatives like tiny homes, and building small homes off the grid. "This area is not receptive to that at all. Each town has their own regulations, but generally it is cost-prohibitive to put a tiny house on a piece of land because land costs are high and it defeats the purpose of trying to save money with a tiny house." Alternative septic options are a non-starter in most towns, she says, "and living off the grid is a big challenge too, all of which are barriers to people trying to cut costs and take housing into their own hands with tiny homes or building off the grid." Lack of municipal water and sewer services means that each home requires land enough to support an on-site water well and waste disposal, adding significantly to costs.

Bradford still has to figure out how to set the stage for the kinds of housing development needed. Master plan surveys show that residents have very different perspectives and preferences when it comes to talk of new housing. "Everyone wants rural, with a town center," Mike James says. But the town has relied on large lot size requirements in rural residential zones to achieve that—which actually results in more suburban sprawl and wasteful consumption of open lands like fields and forests.

■ Generations Work Together to Create Reasons to Stay

Still, the town has been "very supportive of our efforts," Flanders says of the food hub and other younger-generation business development. "Everyone has been really inspired by us younger folks moving home to serve the community and build infrastructure." Food hub member Garrett Bauer served on the town's planning board for two years. He learned a lot from that experience about the protocols for getting projects approved, appropriate signage, and other relevant steps and details that go into building, renovating, or operating a business in town.

"We have been careful to follow the rules and ask for help and guidance when needed, and everyone we have encountered

Keys to Bradford's Community-building Success

- Young people have come together around a sense of purpose and shared core values.
- Intergenerational learning and leadership sharing is key.
- Younger community members value the experience and knowledge of their elders.
- More mature community members listen to the young folks, support their efforts, and welcome them into leadership positions.
- Bringing people together around food fosters communication and respect.

has been very supportive," Flanders emphasizes. "We have actively sought our mentors in areas where we need help—like legality, code enforcement, and town approval.

"They want to see us succeed and they know that the development we are undertaking is good and necessary for the health of Bradford." The group has collaborated closely with other community members, such as the two Mikes who own the Bradford Inn building, to make sure all development is in keeping with their stated values. Flanders concludes, "Having a range of age groups working on this project has helped us to work across age boundaries and get things done for the common good."

The growth of the Kearsarge Food Hub and the way it has led to other new people and new businesses coming to Bradford is both innovative and unique, notes Kathleen Bigford. "People are pretty excited, in a town where things have been pretty flat for a long time." The kids, as she refers to her younger colleagues, are working with the town's new economic development group to put together a packet of information to help prospective new businesses get acquainted with the town, its regulatory policies, and other useful information for a smooth start.

"Bradford is just a town in the middle of nowhere," Mike James observes. "We need to make reasons for people to stay and be part of the community." He feels they are laying the foundation needed to support future positive development. "Bradford is going in a good direction," he asserts.

This truly is a multi-generational initiative, Kathleen Bigford stresses. "This community was ready for it. It's the right idea at the right time. And these particular kids have the right enthusiasm, charisma, and community connections."

Pelham Ditches Restricted-age, Pursues Workforce Housing

5

On March 12, 2019, Pelham, a town of about 14,000 residents tucked in the southeastern corner of Hillsborough County on the Massachusetts border, became the first New Hampshire municipality to repeal restricted-age housing. In their desire to increase equitable and affordable housing options for all ages, the planning board and townspeople didn't stop there.

Having put workforce housing at the top of their agenda for the year, the planning board set a full schedule of community surveys, a two-day planning charrette, and countless meetings to develop plans to increase the supply and diversity of more affordable housing that would be available for people of all ages and different income levels. They engaged consultants to help facilitate the process.

Pelham is one of the faster-growing towns in the state—having grown 9% since the 2010 census count of about 11,000. That's triple the state's overall growth rate of 3% since 2010. The town was incorporated in 1746 and named after Thomas Pelham-Holles, the first Duke of Newcastle. Residents value the historic character and small-town feel of their community and want to ensure that new, denser housing and multi-use development will be compatible. They think it could bring a bonus by livening up the town center area.

The number of dwelling units in Pelham has also grown since 2010, from 4,600 to the current estimated 5,000. The vast majority of homes in the town are owner-occupied. Starting in 1980 Pelham, like many other New Hampshire towns, began permitting the construction of residential condominiums that were age-restricted, meaning only people age 55 or older were eligible to live in them. According to the state Office of Strategic Initiatives 2018 survey of New Hampshire municipalities, 80 communities employ age-restricted housing regulations, "which typically limit residential development in certain areas to persons over age 55 or 62."

By 2019 Pelham had over 300 age-restricted units, including 70 units then under construction—about 6 percent of the town's housing stock. In 2018, Pelham Planning Director Jeff Gowan started to examine the impacts of the increasing number of age-restricted housing units. He found they were really not as "cost-free" to the town as had been promised by advocates—who claimed that since they would produce no children to educate, age-restricted units would be low-cost for the town.

The age-restricted condo units had been granted greater density and other waivers that reduced costs per unit, but also reduced property tax valuations. Furthermore, a not insignificant number of owners of these units had petitioned for elderly property-tax exemptions. The town had not anticipated that the costs of other town services incurred by residents of age-restricted condo units would exceed the reduced assessments from these units. Topping the unanticipated town expenses is increased demand for public safety personnel, especially emergency medical services, beyond the typical residential demand. And savings on school costs? Enrollments had declined, but school taxes had not.

Old Pelham Library and Pelham Historical Society Museum.

Many people in town had supported these age-restricted developments because they thought they would be affordable for older Pelham residents to move into when they were ready to downsize from the larger houses where they had raised their families. But in reality, these age-restricted condominium developments were priced too high for most long-term elder Pelham residents. Older people from Massachusetts—who brought more equity from selling their pricier Bay State homes—bought most of these new condo units.

After analyzing the real costs to the town of age-restricted housing, the Planning Board placed a warrant article on the town ballot in March of 2019 to amend the town's zoning ordinance to stop any future age-restricted housing from being built in Pelham. The warrant article read:

ARTICLE 2: Are you in favor of Amendment No. 1 as proposed by the Planning Board for the Town of Pelham to repeal in its entirety Pelham Zoning Ordinance Article IX,

Elderly Housing? The effect of the repeal would be to eliminate any future age-restricted housing as an allowed use
within Pelham. (Recommended by the Planning Board.)

This was the first proposal by any town or city in New
Hampshire to eliminate any new age-restricted housing. In
most New Hampshire towns, the percentage of voters age 55
or older is now large enough to determine the outcome of any
such vote—if all or most of the age group voted the same way.
In Pelham, nearly half of registered voters are age 55 or older.
But all those senior voters did not vote in opposition to Article 2,
which needed a simple majority of voters at the polls on March
12, 2019, for approval. The article passed by better than a two-
thirds (67.8%) majority: 1,531 to 726.

With that historic vote, an overwhelming majority of voters
in Pelham sent a message that housing that discriminates against
residents under age 55 was not in the best interest of their town.
Discussions among town residents after the vote suggested that
the contest might have been closer had these age-restricted units
been more affordable for long-time Pelham residents and not
acquired mostly by more affluent out-of-state buyers.

Planning Director Jeff Gowan has played a key role in
Pelham's examination of the impacts and unintended consequences of promoting age-restricted housing. He and his
family have lived in Pelham since 1988, and prior to becoming
planning director, he had served on both the Pelham planning
board and zoning board of adjustment. Gowan saw that the
age-restricted housing had made the aging of the area's population worse, making it more difficult for the town and other local
employers to find workers.

Gowan's long commitment to the town and his ability to
bring people together to solve problems helped build consensus
around the idea of changing Pelham's zoning to foster housing

for people of all ages, rather than favoring age-restricted housing. The Pelham Planning Board did not stop with elimination of the town's age-restricted zoning incentives. Looking to take effective actions to create more affordable housing options in their community for people of all ages and income levels, the board made workforce housing their top priority for 2019. They have written a workforce housing ordinance to be put before the voters for approval on the March 2020 town ballot.

■ Finding Ways to Grow Affordable Housing

In May 2019, the Pelham planning board convened a workforce housing design charrette. Pelham residents were invited to participate and discuss when, how, and where they would like to see the development of more affordable workforce housing. Also participating in the charrette were various housing professionals—including representatives from the Workforce Housing Coalition of the Greater Seacoast, architects, engineers, realtors, and mortgage lenders. Town residents worked together with these resource people to identify ways to create financially feasible workforce housing projects. The key objective was to work through various design options with the goal of designing a housing project that was affordable to average income families, as well as economically feasible for the builders and mortgage lenders. Designs also had to be acceptable to local residents and compatible with existing housing and the character of Pelham.

The first part of the two-day charrette was a listening session giving town residents an opportunity to discuss the kinds of workforce housing they would like to see. Attendees expressed a clear desire to maintain the small-town look and feel of their community, and they wanted to be sure that good design principles were incorporated into any architectural plans.

During the charrette, participants discussed many potential locations for affordable housing projects. They identified one available site of just under one acre near the center of Pelham, an area that residents would like to see made more lively with new residential and business activity. One option involved designing a cluster of small cottages, which would be feasible with conventional financing and would also meet current zoning requirements. These cottage homes would meet the needs and preferences for people at all life stages.

However, the charrette participants also found downsides to the chosen site, including the lack of municipal sewer and a lot size too small under current zoning to create the density needed for affordable rental housing or to qualify for tax credits. Thus, another recommendation to come out of the charrette was that the town should amend their zoning ordinance to allow for higher density and smaller lot sizes.

An additional recommendation was that Pelham create a mixed-use zoning district where municipal services would be provided to support higher density and smaller lot sizes. The concept is to create walkable places where people of various stages of life and different income levels could afford and want to live—while ensuring that the location and design remain in keeping with Pelham's rural heritage.

One other important recommendation to come out of the charrette was for Pelham to allow accessory dwelling units (ADUs) to be constructed on a lot where there is now only a single-family dwelling. The idea is that allowing larger accessory units (also known as in-law apartments) and eliminating the owner-occupancy requirement could result in up to hundreds of affordable dwelling units without materially changing the town's character.

Two representatives from the Workforce Housing Coalition of the Greater Seacoast, Executive Director Sarah Wrightsman and Treasurer Michael Castagna of Castagna Consulting, participated in the charrette. Castagna later told the planning board that as he walked through the charrette, he saw that people in Pelham "were pretty much on the same page with regard to the vision to make it work and make the town better." Pelham was ahead of other towns, Castagna said, "because they had a goal and were figuring out steps of how to achieve it."

Wrightsman says she sees in Pelham's residents a "willingness to, one: explore the issue and be part of the solution, and, two: turn their talk into action!" Pelham is among the first New Hampshire communities to repeal the incentives for age-restricted housing, she notes. "Since that monumental vote, Pelham continues to surprise me," Wrightsman adds. "Local leaders were very involved in the planning of the charrette, in the charrette itself, and are pushing forward with amendments to their zoning."

Wrightsman sees the Pelham planning board giving a lot more than just lip service to creating more diverse and affordable housing in town. "At the planning board meeting that I was at, toward the end," she said, "one planning board member was very eager to turn the talk into action. So many communities are happy to keep talking and never translate their good intentions into actual change. Pelham is a very open community."

This important design workshop, with its fancy French name, brought many Pelham residents together for a breakthrough moment. Setting an example for other towns to consider, Pelham's charrette demonstrated that with thoughtful design and placement, residents have nothing to fear—and in fact have much to gain from affordable workforce housing.

The meeting also showed that existing large-lot zoning (one-acre minimum per house in Pelham) was wasteful of land and expensive for homeowners and the town itself. The recommendation to permit more accessory dwelling units addresses that problem in part. The workshop also revealed how affordable housing for people of all ages was far more beneficial to the town than any age-restricted housing that excluded children. One town administration staffer spoke compellingly about how hard it is for town employees to find homes in Pelham that they could afford on their salaries or wages.

Department managers told how hard it is to find employees at all. The most frequently stated benefit for the town of non-discriminatory housing was the potential for more working-age people to live in Pelham—people who could potentially be employed by the school district or any of the municipal departments—or by commercial and service enterprises in town.

Other towns wanting to do what Pelham has done must undertake a willingness to overcome deeply rooted myths around housing diversity, school costs, incentives for elderly housing, and set positive goals and steps to a more sustainable and resilient future. Long-term costs of incentivizing an elderly population while discouraging families with children are very large.

When people exclude workforce housing from their towns and cities in favor of age-restricted housing, they think they are just keeping out children. But they are also changing the social fabric of the community, squeezing vitality out of civic life, and creating both short- and long-term worker shortages damaging to our economic future.

Londonderry Aims to Grow with Places for All Ages

For decades, the town of Londonderry has been one of New Hampshire's faster-growing communities. Famous for its apple orchards, the once-small town now counts more than 25,000 residents. The town's location abutting Manchester—most of Manchester-Boston Regional Airport is actually in Londonderry—and great access to I-93 have conspired to make growth inevitable. The community's long dedication to preserving farms and open space and providing topnotch schools has kept it attractive to families.

In a 2016 interview on NHPR's *Morning Edition*, Londonderry Town Manager Kevin Smith talked about what this growth means for the town. Smith noted that the town's location had brought lots of commercial and industrial growth—with jobs. People want to live close to where they work, he noted, and the good schools are a big draw as well. "The other thing is that as a town in our last master plan, we really made a deliberate attempt to say we want to cover the entire spectrum, from Millennials to seniors, and provide them with the housing opportunities they're looking for. And what's interesting about those two groups is a lot of times they're looking for the same kind of housing. They don't necessarily want to own; they want to be able to rent. They don't need 2,000 square feet, and they want to be able to walk or commute close to where they work or where they shop."

In 2010, Londonderry already saw detrimental impacts from increasingly unbalanced demographics, which were spelled out in the Introduction to the Master Plan adopted that year:

The citizens of Londonderry value its rural character and small-town charm. A great school system and many recreation and sporting opportunities significantly contribute to the quality of life enjoyed by current residents. Additionally, residents and visitors from around New England enjoy the luxuries of Londonderry's expansive natural areas, trail systems, and apple orchards.

Despite all of these amenities, Londonderry is facing some challenges going forward. Demographic data shows that Londonderry's population is disproportionately composed of seniors and elderly citizens. While people in this age cohort have much to offer the community in the way of experience and wisdom, an imbalance in the demographic profile of any community can become unsustainable. Not only is the population of Londonderry aging but there is an abnormally large gap in the population between the ages of 20 to 34, the future leaders within a community.

As a result of the aging population, school enrollment is down, giving the school department the ability to utilize school facilities more efficiently and catch up with much needed improvements. However, residents participating in Planapalooza (Planapalooza is a trade-marked interactive, participatory design and visioning process) expressed concerns regarding the future of public investment in the schools, as a growing segment of residents do not have school-aged children. In Londonderry, a decrease in school funding could be particularly problematic because the superior education and activities offered by the schools appear to be the number one reason that people move to town. The indication from residents interviewed at Planapalooza was that their primary motive to move to Londonderry was the quality school system...

The 2010 Master Plan's guiding principles include staying forever green, promoting unique activity centers, increasing transportation choice and walkability, and emphasizing housing choice and diversity. The plan calls for "a greater range of housing choices to enable a diversity of people at all stages of life to enjoy Londonderry, including young adults, families, retirees, seniors, and people of different income levels. Housing opportunities should include small cottages, dignified multi-family housing, and live-work units, in addition to single-family homes. A more diversified housing strategy will promote affordable housing and a more livable community." The transportation principle stresses "promoting active living for all ages, with special attention given to the mobility of children and seniors."

Since the 2010 Master Plan, the town has seen progress toward the goal of increasing housing supply and diversity, with a number of workforce housing developments, along with a new assisted living center, and some 55-and-up luxury apartments, which Smith said were "making it attractive for both ends of the spectrum." Locals hope that a two-building, 100-unit, subsidized, rent-controlled senior housing development will be affordable for local seniors who are ready to give up maintaining their single-family homes. The town itself approached the developer to create the housing at a former brownfield owned by the town.

Londonderry will continue to grow as the innovative Woodmont Commons development is built out on 600+ acres of former apple orchard. The Woodmont Commons Facebook page describes the billion-dollar New Urbanist development as "a unique urban village amongst the rural country side of Londonderry, NH." By October 2019, the 603 Brewery Beer Hall, among others, was open for business, and the town had issued an occupancy permit for the first completed 87-unit apartment building.

Woodmont Commons is designed by DPZ, the pioneering Smart Growth/New Urbanism firm founded by Andres Duany and Elizabeth Plater-Zyberk to replace suburban sprawl with neighborhood-based planning. The plan features 1,300 new homes, plus commercial and industrial development and community services, to be phased in over 20 years. The village's outer edges will feature detached homes compatible with the adjacent single-family properties. A range of attached dwelling options including townhouses, apartment buildings, and senior housing are being built closer to the village center. The town created a Planned Unit Development Master Plan specific to the Woodmont Commons development.

85

Upper Valley's Regional Collaboration

6

At the crossroads of two interstate highways, amidst the Connecticut River Valley's fertile farmlands, with views of the White Mountains to the east and the Green Mountains to the west, this region's economy is anchored and powered by Dartmouth College and Dartmouth-Hitchcock Health. Those two institutions have spun off dozens of businesses, varying from finance to biomedicine. Some of New Hampshire's best-known manufacturing and tech companies are based here—from Red River in Claremont to Hypertherm in Hanover. Jobs are plentiful.

But there is some trouble in this apparent paradise—the same troubles afflicting other areas of the state and region. The workforce is not expanding to fill all those jobs, and labor shortages have become critical. The region's housing stock has not kept up with demand. Housing supply is so inadequate that new hires have been known to decline accepted positions because they could not find housing.

Dartmouth-Hitchcock Health (D-HH)—New Hampshire's only academic health system and the state's largest private employer—struggles to fill the full range of positions. Sarah Currier, D-HH vice president for workforce strategy, reports

Employees participating in Dartmouth-Hitchcock Health internship programs receive college credits and earn wages while receiving hands-on training for positions such as medical assistant or pharmacy technician.

that over the last year D-HH has consistently carried around 1,000 vacant positions, across all levels of the organization. Currier says D-HH hires 300 people a month, but another 300 positions also open up every month.

However, the Upper Valley brings one big advantage to solving these twin challenges. The people and communities of the Upper Valley region of New Hampshire and Vermont have evolved a habit of shared vision and regional cooperation. The history of cooperation and visionary leadership includes one of the nation's oldest and largest consumer cooperatives, founded as a buying club in 1936 and now known as the Co-op Food Stores. The co-op promotes local farms and foods and has grown to four food stores and two automotive service centers.

Since its founding in 1986, the Upper Valley Land Trust (UVLT) has worked with private landowners, towns, community groups, and conservation partners to strategically and permanently protect working farms and forests, critical habitat and water resources, keystone scenic parcels, and favorite recreational lands and trails. UVLT's leadership, vision and focus over time have helped to make and keep the Upper Valley a special place to live and work. Two cross-border cooperative school districts extend collaboration and relationships across the river— the state line—helping to tie these towns together as neighbors.

Twin Pines Housing was formed in 1990 when two housing organizations with similar visions merged to develop and provide affordable housing for low- and moderate-income families in the Upper Valley. Twin Pines is the only non-profit providing multi-family affordable housing in a service area spanning northern Windsor and southeastern Orange Counties, in Vermont, and southern Grafton and northern Sullivan Counties, in New Hampshire. Since 1990, Twin Pines Housing has developed or purchased a variety of housing—including apartments, mobile-home lots, single-family homes, and condominiums.

Since 1994, Vital Communities, a 501c nonprofit organization serving 69 communities of the Upper Valley region in two states, has worked to make the region more vibrant and more connected, by bringing citizens, organizations, and municipalities together "to address issues where an independent voice and regional approach are essential." The organization, with $1.3 million in annual revenue, leads many programs focused on cultivating the local economy, local knowledge, and sense of place for all ages, as described at the website www.vitalcommunities.org. The Vital Communities purpose:

Vital Communities is a nonprofit organization that cultivates the civic, environmental, and economic vitality of the Upper Valley. We bring people together, bridging boundaries and engaging our whole community to create positive change.

Tree-huggers and Developers

Betty Porter's vision of the potential for the towns of the Upper Valley to work together sparked the founding of the Vital Communities organization. She has said the most important vision for what has become Vital Communities was the need for a "neutral convener." "Because when you've got people who are developers and people who are tree-huggers," she explains, "you can't get them talking together if you're seen as an advocate for either party."

Porter decided to take action after reading a *Valley News* editorial in 1993 that encouraged readers to "think of themselves not only as residents of an individual town or state, but of a region" and to "think about preserving the qualities that make the Upper Valley a desirable place to live."

On behalf of the Vital Communities 25-member Corporate Council, three leaders—Clay Adams, chair and Mascoma Bank president and CEO; Tom Roberts, Vital Communities executive director; and Mike Kiess, Vital Communities workforce housing coordinator—penned an op-ed for the *Valley News* in January 2019:

Fixing the housing shortage in our region requires ideas and action from current residents, civic leaders and organizations. We are a volunteer group of this region's largest and best-known institutions, businesses and non-profits. Collectively, we employ more than 16,000 people and reach well over half the households in the Upper Valley. We are deeply committed to strengthening our region. Chief among our concerns is making sure local people can continue to afford to live here...We worry that when employees, especially younger employees with families, have to commute long distances, they are less available to participate in school activities and local governance. They are farther from childcare, healthcare and all of the interactions that make community and family life stronger. By acting together as neighbors and communities, we can create more places to live that support our environment, our culture and all that we value in the Upper Valley.

Vital Communities is working to raise awareness of the complex social and economic impacts of the housing shortage. "When residents live and work in the same community, there are lasting positive impacts," the website explains:

People have more time to be involved in civic life, support local businesses, and invest themselves in the long-term health of the community. They save money and reduce environmental impacts from commuting. Local employers benefit, too, when their employees have stable housing they can afford.

■ Who Will Prepare the Operating Rooms?

More than 12,000 permanent, full- and part-time employees at D-HH locations in New Hampshire and Vermont serve a population of 1.9 million across northern New England, providing care throughout New Hampshire and Vermont. The flagship Dartmouth-Hitchcock Medical Center in Lebanon employs more than 5,000. Seventy-five percent of all D-HH employees live in New Hampshire.

Workforce matters. "No job is unimportant in health care," D-HH's Currier notes:

> You think if you have the surgeons, you can perform the surgeries. But in reality, it takes so much more than that. If you don't have enough perioperative support staff (special operating room housekeepers), you can't flip an operating room. You can have the surgeons, and the space—but still be waiting if you don't have someone to make sure the space is ready.

The hospital has had to turn away people needing surgery. Patients have also been turned away when patient rooms cannot be prepared in time, she adds, because beds are not ready. "We don't want to ever do that. Nurses, doctors, LNAs, housekeepers—every person who works here is an important part of the ecosystem. We need them ALL," she wrote in an email.

■ Getting Creative in Workforce Development and Housing

Currier urges more employers to get involved in local housing efforts. "We didn't think we had a voice in local matters," she says, "but now we do." Upper Valley employers have gotten very creative—developing their own workforce and getting housing built. They are making sure students in local middle and high schools are aware of the career opportunities available at the dynamic industries and institutions right in their backyards. "The segment that has been missed are those not choosing to go to college," notes Carolyn Isabelle, manager of workforce strategy for D-HH. "They need pathways not just for jobs, but for life." The workforce strategy team is finding ways to help individuals at whatever age get skills they need to launch meaningful careers.

D-HH has created internship programs for positions such as medical assistant and pharmacy technician. Interns earn college credits and are paid for their training time. Jasmin Johnson, now a medical assistant with D-HH Primary Care, applied for the internship program as a senior in high school. She's the third person in her family to complete the program. "The program really helped me figure out what I wanted to do," Johnson says. She had wanted to pursue a nursing degree after high school, but fearing the cost and the debt, she decided against college. Now she's going to college—with the help of D-HH's tuition assistance program. The apprenticeship and tuition assistance programs have allowed her to work, earn college credits, and save money toward her goal of her own home.

The Corporate Council has led to more networking. The group hosts a Business Leaders Breakfast on Housing each spring and fall. Employers are collaborating on recruiting and workforce development, as well as on housing. Instead of competing, they are helping each other find prospective workers. Currier says that D-HH and Hypertherm, for example, help each other because employees at one organization are likely to have spouses or other family members or friends who could benefit from opportunities at the other.

In the iconic college town of Hanover, housing has been high-priced and in short supply for decades. Dartmouth professors have been unable to find or afford homes. To help faculty and staff find housing, Dartmouth College has gone into the real estate business. The college now owns and manages 540 on- and off-campus rental-housing units within two miles of campus. The college offers these homes—ranging from studio apartments to single-family homes—to graduate students while pursuing their degrees, and to full-time faculty and staff as transitional housing for up to three years.

Twin Pines Housing recently completed a 24-unit affordable housing development in Hanover, called Summer Park Residences, for seniors and persons with disabilities. The energy-efficient apartments are fully accessible, elevator-equipped, in a building built to passive house standards, and outfitted with photovoltaic panels to generate energy.

The towns and cities of the Upper Valley are diverse, each with its own distinct character, challenges, and aspirations. The many small towns have long relied on the larger, more developed communities like the cities of Lebanon and Claremont to provide most of the housing diversity for the region. All the communities in the region are grappling with the need for more housing of all types, and in New Hampshire, with changing state laws designed to support more affordable housing. These include the laws governing accessory dwelling units and the creation of the Housing Appeals Board.

But these towns can draw on the strength and connections of their established regional working relationships. As Vital Communities describes, *"When our communities work together, we find innovative ways to move forward on the challenges we all face."* Through their partnership with Vital Communities and the Corporate Council, D-HH is exploring the possibility of partnering with developers to construct apartment blocks near the Dartmouth-Hitchcock Medical Center on some of the expansive woodland owned by D-HH that surrounds the hospital campus. Repurposing existing buildings is another possibility.

First-in-the-nation Rural Geriatric Emergency Department

The largely rural setting of northern New England, one of the nation's most rapidly aging regions, offers unique obstacles to implementing improved acute care for the growing population of senior adults, according to Dartmouth-Hitchcock Health. The region's largest healthcare provider network announced plans in October 2019 to create the nation's first geriatric emergency department dedicated to serving rural areas.

"As the US population ages, older adults are turning to emergency departments (EDs) for their health care needs," D-HH explained in a press release. "In response, EDs must be equipped not only to deal with acute medical emergencies, but also to coordinate care, avoid admissions when possible, provide patients with support, and connect them to community partners through an ED environment designed with the needs of seniors in mind."

To create an innovative "Geriatric Emergency Department" (GED), Dartmouth-Hitchcock Health will partner with the West Health family of nonprofit and nonpartisan organizations dedicated to lowering health care costs to enable seniors to successfully age in place. The GED will have protocols, resources, and specialized care areas to optimize acute care of older adults. Most hospital GEDs have been in urban or larger academic medical centers. The D-HH/West Health collaboration will be the first in the nation to focus on a largely rural population. D-HH said the combination of West Health's expertise in geriatric medicine and D-HH's pioneering telehealth and geriatrics experience will allow the GED to serve older acute-care patients throughout the region through D-HH's hub-and-spoke system with regional hospitals.

Conclusion:
What About the Future?

L oss of population in rural areas is a concern for many states and regions across the country. New Hampshire's demographic challenges are different. Nine of its 10 counties are expected to continue growing, albeit modestly. But much of that growth consists of an influx of older residents, as was reported in an article by Gretchen Grosky, health and aging reporter for the *Union Leader* in September 2016. According to projections from the state Office of Energy and Planning (now Office of Strategic Initiatives), by 2040 one-out-of-three Granite Staters will be 65 or older. Compare that to 2018, when 18% of the New Hampshire population was 65 or over.

State officials and their consultants have estimated that by 2040 there will be about 400,000 residents 65 or older—more than double the number counted in the 2010 Census. The number of residents 85 years and older is projected to exceed 85,000, more than triple the 25,000 in the 2010 Census. The report projects further declines in children under age 15 from 2010 to 2040, with the under-15 portion of the population falling from 17.6% to 15%.

Low fertility levels for the relatively large Millennial generation are projected to result in slightly declining births. But deaths will increase sharply due to the aging of the Baby Boom generation. By 2040, all 10 New Hampshire counties are projected to experience more deaths than births. The northern New England states are discovering that the challenges posed by increasing numbers of old people are compounded by the simultaneous decrease in numbers of younger people. The ranks of working-age adults have not kept up with the workforce needs throughout the economy, but especially in health and elder care. Finding caregivers, medical and support staff is becoming a very serious problem.

The 2016 State and County Population Projections report, which can be found on the State Office of Strategic Initiatives website, notes that "while this is a likely scenario, many factors can alter the course of future events...This is not a prediction of future population but rather the population outcome if the assumptions about future fertility, mortality, and migration occur in the future." The people of New Hampshire can bend this trajectory by making changes in our communities, investing in public education from pre-K to graduate school, and by collaborating with neighboring communities, to make New Hampshire a more age-friendly place—for all ages.

Towns and cities in New Hampshire responded mightily to the perceived need for housing among the senior population. More housing and more housing choices are needed as the population ages—and as more older people choose to move here. But we have created an artificial distinction with age-segregated living. The communities we admire and celebrate are traditional communities, both rural and urban, not only of mixed uses, but mixed incomes and mixed generations. We have more recently evolved housing patterns that are not like that, and we are now frustrated by some of the outcomes.

In his now-classic book, *Bowling Alone: The Collapse and Revival of American Community*, Robert Putnam, a New

Hampshire resident and Harvard professor of public policy, shows how changes in work, family structure, age, suburban life, technology, women's roles and other factors have contributed to declines in community life and connectedness. As people are forced to seek affordable housing at ever-greater distances from their jobs, they spend more time commuting, less time with family and friends. Fewer people are able to volunteer with local organizations or serve on town boards. Further segregation of communities by age and income will not help.

The history of human civilization is fraught with examples where people believed in myths that drove decisions with serious, even fatal consequences. For 30 years, many towns and cities have made decisions to discourage or deny permits for workforce housing, while encouraging age-restricted housing. These development policies have succeeded all too well in their intent to limit or exclude families with children. The results are fewer students, workers, shoppers and community volunteers—and limiting economic and civic activity.

We are learning that each community needs more young people to renew the labor force as older residents retire or are no longer able to work. New Hampshire's rapidly rising cohorts of aged residents need a full array of labor-intensive health and support services. No group has a greater interest in the presence of working-age adults than the aging. In favoring the old, communities are inadvertently diminishing the care and services available for the elderly. A decade ago, a friend in her 90s said she knew this demographic imbalance meant trouble when she moved into the county nursing home and saw that "all the nurses and aides were grandmothers."

That's why AARP is promoting age-friendly communities that appeal to and integrate all ages. Communities AARP describes as "age-friendly" appeal to Millennials and their grandparents. All want walkable streets, housing and transportation options, access to key services, and opportunities to participate in community life. AARP's Age-Friendly Community Network encourages "states, cities, towns and counties to prepare for the rapid aging of the US population by paying increased attention to the environmental, economic and social factors that influence the health and well-being of older adults. By doing so, these communities are better equipped to become great places, and even lifelong homes, for people of all ages."

High costs for land and homes in New England are a challenge, but local zoning can be revisited to root out obstacles designed to limit development of workforce or affordable housing. Large lot-size minimums can be replaced with science-based lot-size-by-soil-type zoning. Zoning to promote mixed-use development can create desirable, walkable communities, and promote commercial tax-base growth along with denser and more varied residential construction.

In Bradford, Lancaster, Pelham, the Upper Valley and other places, people of all generations are working together to revitalize and strengthen communities and institutions. Newcomers are working with lifelong residents. Schools, colleges, towns and cities, organizations and businesses are collaborating. Everyone has a role in rebalancing our human ecology. Ambitious projects can show middle school and high school students career opportunities and pathways awaiting them in their home region. Townspeople can work together to create trail networks, preserve special open spaces and parks, and to support high quality education and childcare opportunities.

Everyone can help roll out the welcome wagon by extending a hand to the young and to newcomers in the community or workplace and making them feel welcome.

Every town or city has a stake in navigating through this demographic turbulence and can determine how best to help bring about a more balanced local and state age structure. New

Hampshire has a long tradition of motivated people in strong, inclusive communities, coming together and finding creative ways to accomplish astonishing things.

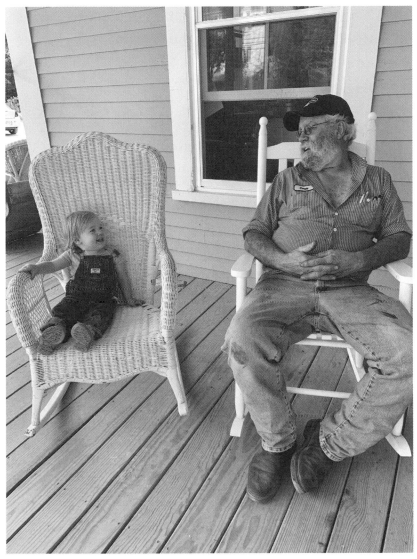

Friends and neighbors, Charlotte Flanders and Bruce Caswell relax on the front porch of the Sweet Beet Market in Bradford.

Appendix:
Resource Toolkit

■ Where to Find Help and Information:

■ **New Hampshire Housing Finance Authority**

New Hampshire Housing promotes, finances, and supports affordable housing for Granite State residents. The agency offers safe, fixed-rate mortgages; rental assistance for low-income families and individuals; and financing for the development of quality, affordable rental housing. Data, resources, and planning information includes Accessory Dwelling Unit Guides for homeowners and municipalities.

- General information: https://www.nhhfa.org
- Contact: comments@nhhfa.org;
  (603) 472-8623 | (800) 640-7239

■ **New Hampshire Association of Regional Planning Commissions (NHARPC)**

NHARPC is the affiliation of the nine regional planning commissions (RPCs) in the state of New Hampshire. Regional planning commissions are required by New Hampshire statute to prepare regional master plans, compile housing needs assessments, and review developments of regional impact.

NHARPC coordinates the activities of the RPCs on a statewide basis by providing information and technical assistance to its members and other groups and organizations. It maintains strategic partnerships with various state and federal agencies and develops planning policies, programs, legislative positions, responses to topical issues, and special projects and initiatives working on behalf of its member commissions and, by extension, the member cities and towns across New Hampshire.

- Find your RPC on the NHARPC website:
  http://www.nharpc.org

■ **AARP—Age-Friendly and Livable Communities**

AARP's mission is to empower people to choose how they live as they age.

- https://www.aarp.org/livable-communities/archives
  /info-2014/housing.html

■ **AARP—New Hampshire**

- General information:
  https://states.aarp.org/new-hampshire/
- Contact: nh@aarp.org; (866) 542-8168

■ **New Hampshire Office of Strategic Initiatives (OSI)**

Formerly the Office of State Planning, Office of Energy & Planning, OSI provides information, data, and guidance to assist decision-makers on issues pertaining to development, land protection, energy use, and community planning. They guide the state's future growth through public policy development, education, research, and partnership building.

- General information: https://www.nh.gov/osi/

■ **Stay Work Play New Hampshire**

**"Encouraging More Young Workers to Stay
Work and Play in New Hampshire."**

New Hampshire is a great state in which to live, ranking very highly in terms of health, safety, low taxes, personal income, and livability. Most individuals who attend college here or visit from another state recall positive experiences vacationing or exploring New Hampshire. They also want to stay or return here later in life. But currently, only about half of the state's college graduates actually do stay.

The goal of Stay Work Play NH is to expose more young people to the advantages of remaining in or returning to New Hampshire.

- General information: https://stayworkplay.org
- Contact: (603)860-2245

For the results of the December 2017 survey of 20–40-year-olds, visit https://stayworkplay.org/survey/.

■ **New Hampshire Municipal Association (NHMA)**

NHMA is a non-profit, non-partisan membership association established in 1941. It is a member-funded, member-governed, and member-driven association that works to strengthen New Hampshire cities and towns and enhance their ability to serve the public. Through the collective power of cities and towns, NHMA promotes effective municipal government by providing education, training, advocacy and legal services.

Town & City magazine September/October 2019 articles include LEGAL Q&A: "What Municipalities Need to Know About 'Workforce Housing'" and "When is a House a Hotel?"

- General information: www.nhmunicipal.org
- Contact: (603) 224-7447

■ New Hampshire Preservation Alliance / Heritage and Historic Preservation

Community Revitalization Tax Incentive RSA 79-E is a state law that encourages investment in downtowns and village centers. It provides a tax incentive for the rehabilitation and active use of under-utilized commercial buildings and, in so doing, aims to promote strong local economies and smart, sustainable growth as an alternative to sprawl. The tax incentive must be adopted at the local level before it can be offered to property-owners.

For more information on this state incentive program, including a fact sheet and flow chart, visit the New Hampshire Preservation Alliance (NHPA) website https://nhpreservation.org/commercial-property-79e, or contact the NHPA directly.

- General information: https://nhpreservation.org
- Contact: admin@nhpreservation.org; (603) 224-2281
- Address:
  New Hampshire Preservation Alliance
  7 Eagle Square
  PO Box 268
  Concord, NH 03302-0268

■ New Hampshire Division of Historical Resources

The mission of the Division of Historical Resources is to preserve and celebrate New Hampshire's irreplaceable historic resources through programs and services that provide education, stewardship, and protection.

- General information: https://www.nh.gov/nhdhr/
- Contact: (603) 271-3483

■ **Land and Community Heritage Investment Program (LCHIP)**

"Protecting New Hampshire's Natural, Historic and Cultural Resources."

Since 2000, LCHIP has awarded $37 million and protected:

- 218 Historic Structures Preserved or Revitalized
- Over 283,000 Total Acres Preserved

In this time, LCHIP has made 376 individual grants that positively impacted 150 New Hampshire communities.

- General information: https://lchip.org

■ **University of New Hampshire Cooperative Extension**

Local offices in every county.

- General information: https://extension.unh.edu
- Statewide contact: answers@unh.edu; (877) 398-4769

Specialized interests:

- Community and Economic Development
  General information:
  https://extension.unh.edu/topics/community-economic
  -development
- Preserving Rural Character through Agriculture: A Resource Kit
  for Planners
  General information:
  https://extension.unh.edu/resource/preserving-rural
  -character-through-agriculture-resource-kit-planners-toolkit
- Local Regulation of Agriculture Toolkit
  General information:
  https://extension.unh.edu/blog/3-ways-make-your-community
  -farm-friendly
- Creating an Agricultural Commission in Your Hometown
  General information:
  https://extension.unh.edu/resources/files
  /Resource000021_Rep21.pdf

■ New Hampshire Department of Agriculture, Markets & Food

The mission of the New Hampshire Department of Agriculture, Markets & Food is to support and promote agriculture and serve consumers and business for the benefit of the public health, environment and economy. Get information on farmers markets, local farms and foods, agritourism, and more.

- General information: https://www.agriculture.nh.gov

- Contact: (603) 271-3551

■ University of New Hampshire Carsey School of Public Policy

"Northern New Hampshire Youth in a Changing Economy"

A decade-long study of Coos County youth by the University of New Hampshire Carsey School of Public Policy (access full report at https://carsey.unh.edu/new-hampshire) surveyed and did in-depth interviews with youth over several years. The research team wanted to understand how young people are affected by the changing economy, what influences their decisions to leave the region or stay, and what draws back those who return. They sought to help North Country communities to support their young people and thereby build a new future.

This study has relevance for youth and communities in other areas of New Hampshire beyond the North Country region.

The Carsey study found in Coos County a persistently strong sense of community, including trust and cooperation, and that all this matters to teens. "We know that teachers and mentors matter. And we know that both the sense of community and the support of caring adults make a difference for young people, including, importantly, for those in stressed and chaotic families," concludes the report. The report finds that "Youth who feel like their voices are heard during childhood and adolescence may be more prone to desire a long-term future in Coos even if they leave for a while during early adulthood to pursue educational or professional opportunities elsewhere."

The sense of community among Coos youth is strong and remained resilient in the face of the Great Recession. The exception is youth voice, which remained low in comparison to school belonging, community integration, and community support.

Dr. Eleanor Jaffee, who managed the study, says those with a strong sense of community did better. "Their well-being, in terms of future mental health and substance use and also their desire to return to the region in the future, all kind of revolves around this idea of community attachment."

Despite this, youth reported not having a voice in community decision-making.

"Young people did not feel like they had a seat at the table in talking about the future of the region," Jaffee notes, "And that's where we feel like there's maybe some work to do."

■ New Hampshire Listens

New Hampshire Listens is a civic engagement initiative of the Carsey School of Public Policy at the University of New Hampshire. In the same way that we need the physical infrastructure of roads, bridges, and buildings, we need to build, strengthen, and sustain civic infrastructure to support a strong democracy. The mission of New Hampshire Listens is to help New Hampshire residents talk and work together to create communities that work for everyone.

- General information:
  https://carsey.unh.edu/new-hampshire-listens

■ What is New Hampshire?

What is New Hampshire? was originally an annual publication of the New Hampshire Center for Public Policy Studies, now produced by the Carsey School of Public Policy.

The purpose of *What is New Hampshire?* is to set a factual baseline of understanding as the state makes decisions about its future. It is not meant to prove any particular points, or to support any particular opinions regarding the choices to be made by the state's governments, people or businesses. It is a set of facts and simple descriptive text describing where we are, where we have been, and what challenges we may face based on our analysis. It is our hope that by starting from a common factual premise, discussion in the state will be elevated and the decisions will be made on the basis of a deeper understanding of the underlying facts.

- General information:
  https://carsey.unh.edu/what-is-new-hampshire

■ Will More Kids in Town Raise the Local Tax Rate?

Will More Kids in Town Raise the Local Tax Rate? is an August 15, 2019, report to the New Hampshire Realtors Association by Richard W. England, PhD, Professor Emeritus of Economics at the University of New Hampshire Paul College of Business and Economics. Includes analysis of school enrollments and tax rates for all 234 cities and towns and 167 school districts.

- Access the paper at: www.nhar.org/kids

■ Kennebunkport Heritage Housing Trust (KHHT)

A group of Kennebunkport, Maine, residents recently formed the nonprofit Kennebunkport Heritage Housing Trust (KHHT) to address the acute need for workforce or affordable housing in this town of 3,585 residents. Maine is the only state with a higher median age than New Hampshire. The York County coastal community faces similar challenges to neighboring towns in New Hampshire's Seacoast region and other tourism-influenced areas. Widening gaps between median incomes and median home prices have kept non-waterfront homes in Kennebunkport out of reach for young families or local seniors looking to downsize. From 2000 to 2019, the median house cost in Kennebunkport doubled from $234,200 to $481,637. However, during the same time, the median household income rose just 41%—from $54,219 to $76,643.

KHHT aims to build 25 homes by 2025, with the first five built in 2020. The three-bedroom homes are intended to attract younger families to live and maybe volunteer in Kennebunkport. KHHT expects a starting cost of $240,000. KHHT's mission is "Creating and sustaining affordable housing for year-round residents to live, work, volunteer and retire in Kennebunkport."

Currently just 56% of Kennebunkport homes are occupied year-round, and that number is shrinking. With fewer younger people in the area during the winter, safety for residents becomes a concern, KHHT board members Jim Fitzgerald and Sue Ellen Stavrand told the *Journal-Tribune* newspaper. "The average age of the volunteer fire department is 55," Stavrand said. "Thirty-five percent are over 60."

The homes will have high quality standards and be guaranteed affordable for younger families. The Kennebunkport group borrowed ideas from similar programs in Bar Harbor, Maine, and Martha's Vineyard, Massachusetts. Qualifying homebuyers will only buy the homes—KHHT will own the land, and lease it to the homeowners. By continuing to hold the land KHHT will prevent values from skyrocketing.

"You can't turn around and flip it, can't turn it into an Airbnb," Fitzgerald explained. Homeowners must meet income requirements, and remain year-round Kennebunkport residents. They are not required to work in Kennebunkport, but the hope is they will jump in and volunteer, get involved in the community.

According to the KHHT website, "A big part of what makes Kennebunkport special is the people, those born here and those who have discovered all we have to offer. The fishermen, local business owners, teachers, firefighters, neighbors, and even a president have woven themselves into the fabric of our community. Our goal is to sustain our year-round mix of residents by supporting homes for families who contribute to the flavor that makes our 'Port so spectacular."

- General information: www.khht.org
- Contact: infokhht@gmail.com

Index

Charts and figures are indicated by page numbers followed by *c* and *f* respectively.

About the Authors

LORRAINE STUART MERRILL has written about agriculture, land use, community planning, business, and the environment in New Hampshire and the Northeast for more than 30 years. She has been a teacher, school board member, and a trustee of the University System of New Hampshire. In 10 years as New Hampshire Commissioner of Agriculture, Markets & Food, Lorraine traveled the state speaking to groups and visiting farms and food businesses. Longtime farmers, she and her husband, John, have two sons and three granddaughters. They received the American Farmland Trust Steward of the Land Award in 2003 for "outstanding leadership at the national, state, and local levels in protecting farmland and caring for the environment." Lorraine is a University of New Hampshire graduate and was a W. K. Kellogg Foundation Food & Society Policy Fellow.

PETER FRANCESE founded *American Demographics Magazine* and often speaks and writes on today's demographically related issues. Francese has written several books on marketing and the impact of demographic trends. He was the co-author with Lorraine Stuart Merrill on the 2008 book and on the documentary by Jay Childs titled *Communities & Consequences: The unbalancing of New Hampshire's Human Ecology and what we can do about it.*

Francese is the recipient of the Silver Bell Award from the Advertising Council for distinguished public service and is a graduate of Cornell University. Francese subsequently served a term on Cornell President's council to provide insight on relevant demographic trends. Francese is a resident of Exeter with his wife, The Honorable Paula Francese, who recently served Exeter for two terms in the New Hampshire House of Representatives. Paula and Peter have three children and five grandchildren. Email contact for this author: peter@francese.com.